POPULAR
MUSIC

The Popular Music Series

Popular Music, 1980–1989 is a revised cumulation of and supersedes Volumes 9 through 14 of the *Popular Music* series, all of which are still available:

Volume 9, 1980–84	Volume 12, 1987
Volume 10, 1985	Volume 13, 1988
Volume 11, 1986	Volume 14, 1989

Popular Music, 1920–1979 is also a revised cumulation of and supersedes Volumes 1 through 8 of the *Popular Music* series, of which Volumes 6 through 8 are still available:

Volume 1, 2nd ed., 1950–59	Volume 5, 1920–29
Volume 2, 1940–49	Volume 6, 1965–69
Volume 3, 1960–64	Volume 7, 1970–74
Volume 4, 1930–39	Volume 8, 1975–79

Popular Music, 1900–1919 is a companion volume to the revised cumulation.

This series continues with:

Volume 15, 1990	Volume 18, 1993
Volume 16, 1991	Volume 19, 1994
Volume 17, 1992	Volume 20, 1995

Other Books by Bruce Pollock

The Face of Rock and Roll: Images of a Generation

Hipper Than Our Kids?: A Rock and Roll Journal of the Baby Boom Generation

In Their Own Words: Popular Songwriting, 1955–1974

When Rock Was Young: The Heyday of Top 40

When the Music Mattered: Rock in the 1960s

ISSN 0886-442X

VOLUME 20

1995

POPULAR MUSIC

An Annotated Guide to American Popular Songs,
Including Introductory Essay, Lyricists and Composers Index,
Important Performances Index,
Awards Index, and List of Publishers

BRUCE POLLOCK
Editor

GALE

Bruce Pollock, *Editor*

Gale Research Inc. Staff

Jolen Marya Gedridge, *Associate Editor*
Lawrence W. Baker, *Managing Editor*

Mary Beth Trimper, *Production Director*
Deborah L. Milliken, *Production Assistant*

Cynthia Baldwin, *Production Design Manager*
Barbara J. Yarrow, *Graphic Services Supervisor*

Theresa Rocklin, *Manager, Technical Support Services*
Shelia Printup, *Programmer/Analyst*

This book is printed on acid-free paper that meets the minimum requirements of American National Standard for Information Sciences—Permanence Paper for Printed Library Materials, ANSI Z39.48-1984.

Library of Congress Catalog Card Number 85-653754
ISBN 0-8103-6428-X
ISSN 0886-442X

10 9 8 7 6 5 4 3 2 1

Contents

About the Book and How to Use It

This volume is the twentieth of a series whose aim is to set down in permanent and practical form a selective, annotated list of the significant popular songs of our times. Other indexes of popular music have either dealt with special areas, such as jazz or theater and film music, or been concerned chiefly with songs that achieved a degree of popularity as measured by the music-business trade indicators, which vary widely in reliability.

Annual Publication Schedule

The first nine volumes in the *Popular Music* series covered sixty-five years of song history in increments of five or ten years. Volume 10 initiated a new annual publication schedule, making background information available as soon as possible after a song achieves prominence. Yearly publication also allows deeper coverage—approximately five hundred songs—with additional details about writers' inspiration, uses of songs, album appearances, and more.

Indexes Provide Additional Access

Three indexes make the valuable information in the song listings even more accessible to users. The Lyricists & Composers Index shows all the songs represented in *Popular Music, 1995,* that are credited to a given individual. The Important Performances Index tells at a glance which albums, musicals, films, television shows, or other media-featured songs are represented in the volume. The "Performer" category—first added to the index as "Vocalist" in the 1986 volume—allows the user to see with which songs an artist has been associated this year. The index is arranged by broad media category, then alphabetically by the show or album title, with the songs listed under each title. Finally, the Awards Index provides a list of the songs nominated for awards by the American Academy of Motion Picture Arts and Sciences (Academy Award) and the American Academy of Recording Arts and Sciences (Grammy Award). Winning songs are indicated by asterisks.

About the Book and How to Use It

List of Publishers

The List of Publishers is an alphabetically arranged directory providing addresses—when available—for the publishers of the songs represented in *Popular Music, 1995*. Also noted is the organization handling performance rights for the publisher—in the United States, the American Society of Composers, Authors, and Publishers (ASCAP) or Broadcast Music, Inc. (BMI); in Canada, the Society of Composers, Authors, and Music Publishers of Canada (SOCAN); and in Europe, the Society of European Songwriters and Composers (SESAC).

Tracking Down Information on Songs

Unfortunately, the basic records kept by the active participants in the music business are often casual, inaccurate, and transitory. There is no single source of comprehensive information about popular songs, and those sources that do exist do not publish complete material about even the musical works with which they are directly concerned. Four of the primary proprietors of basic information about our popular music are the major performing rights societies—ASCAP, BMI, SOCAN, and SESAC. Although each of these organizations has considerable information about the songs of its own writer and publisher members and has also issued indexes of its own songs, their files and published indexes are designed primarily for clearance identification by the commercial users of music. Their publications of annual or periodic lists of their "hits" necessarily include only a small fraction of their songs, and the facts given about these are also limited. ASCAP, BMI, SOCAN, and SESAC are, however, invaluable and indispensable sources of data about popular music. It is just that their data and special knowledge are not readily accessible to the researcher.

Another basic source of information about musical compositions and their creators and publishers is the Copyright Office of the Library of Congress. A computerized file lists each published, unpublished, republished, and renewed copyright of songs registered with the Office. It takes between six months and a year from the time of application before songs are officially registered (in some cases, songs have already been released before copyright registration begins). This file is helpful in determining the precise date of the declaration of the original ownership of musical works, but since some authors, composers, and publishers have been known to employ rather makeshift methods of protecting their works legally, there are songs listed in *Popular Music* that may not be found in the Library of Congress files.

About the Book and How to Use It

Selection Criteria

In preparing the original volumes for this time period, the editor was faced with a number of separate problems. The first and most important of these was that of selection. The stated aim of the project—to offer the user as comprehensive and accurate a listing of significant popular songs as possible—has been the guiding criterion. The purpose has never been to offer a judgment on the quality of any songs or to indulge a prejudice for or against any type of popular music. Rather, it is the purpose of *Popular Music* to document those musical works that (1) achieved a substantial degree of popular acceptance, (2) were exposed to the public in especially notable circumstances, or (3) were accepted and given important performances by influential musical and dramatic artists.

Another problem was whether or not to classify the songs as to type. Most works of music are subject to any number of interpretations and, although it is possible to describe a particular performance, it is more difficult to give a musical composition a label applicable not only to its origin but to its subsequent musical history. In fact, the most significant versions of some songs are often quite at variance with their origins. Citations for such songs in *Popular Music* indicate the important facts about not only their origins but also their subsequent lives, rather than assigning an arbitrary and possibly misleading label.

Research Sources

The principal sources of information for the titles, authors, composers, publishers, and dates of copyright of the songs in this volume were the Copyright Office of the Library of Congress, ASCAP, BMI, SOCAN, SESAC, and individual writers and publishers. Data about best-selling recordings were obtained principally from three of the leading music business trade journals—*Billboard, Radio & Records,* and *Cash Box.* For the historical notes; information about foreign, folk, public domain, and classical origins; and identification of theatrical, film, and television introducers of songs, the editor relied upon collections of album notes, theater programs, sheet music, newspaper and magazine articles, and other material, both his own and that in the Lincoln Center Library for the Performing Arts in New York City.

Contents of a Typical Entry

The primary listing for a song includes

- Title and alternate title(s)
- Country of origin (for non-U.S. songs)

- Author(s) and composer(s)
- Current publisher, copyright date
- Annotation on the song's origins or performance history

Title: The full title and alternate title or titles are given exactly as they appear on the Library of Congress copyright record or, in some cases, the sheet music. Since even a casual perusal of the book reveals considerable variation in spelling and punctuation, it should be noted that these are the colloquialisms of the music trade. The title of a given song as it appears in this series is, in almost all instances, the one under which it is legally registered.

Foreign Origin: If a song is of foreign origin, the primary listing indicates the country of origin after the title. Additional information may be noted, such as the original title, copyright date, writer, publisher in country of origin, or other facts about the adaptation.

Authorship: In all cases, the primary listing reports the author or authors and the composer or composers. The reader may find variations in the spelling of a songwriter's name. This results from the fact that some writers used different forms of their names at different times or in connection with different songs. In addition to this kind of variation in the spelling of writers' names, the reader will also notice that in some cases, where the writer is also the performer, the name as a writer may differ from the form of the name used as a performer.

Publisher: The current publisher is listed. Since *Popular Music* is designed as a practical reference work rather than an academic study, and since copyrights more than occasionally change hands, the current publisher is given instead of the original holder of the copyright. If a publisher has, for some reason, copyrighted a song more than once, the years of the significant copyright subsequent to the year of the original copyright are also listed after the publisher's name.

Annotation: The primary listing mentions significant details about the song's history—the musical, film, or other production in which the song was introduced or featured and, where important, by whom it was introduced, in the case of theater and film songs; any other performers identified with the song; first or best-selling recordings and album inclusions, indicating the performer and the record company; awards; and other relevant data. The name of a performer may be listed differently in connection with different songs, especially over a period of years. The name listed is the form of the name given in connection with a particular performance or record. Dates are provided for important recordings and performances.

Popular Music in 1995

On the pop culture ropes for much of the 90s, the Top 40 as both a radio format and a national artistic and commercial determinant ceased to matter in 1995. The historic sound of the mainstream since 1958—and at the time an ingenious, infectious, insidious messenger of teen arcana and the big beat—the Top 40 was done in this year by a lack of the very rock and roll it had been its original mission to champion.

Ironically, 1995's Top 40 was dominated by approximately 70% to 30% by rhythm and blues-based dance, rap, and hip-hop over the guitar-driven, country-inspired, self-contained band units that once brought Elvis Presley and Buddy Holly to prominence and the Top 40 its initial glory years. Having feasted on the carcass of rhythm and blues at that time, paying lip service to its sweating legends while burying them in paupers' graves, the ghosts of rock and roll are now surely twirling in agony at the spectacle of being squeezed off the charts by those who have waited nearly forty years in the shadows to reclaim what may have been rightfully theirs in the first place. And yet, in another bizarre twist, these new-fashioned descendants of R&B found themselves in a position much like a modern day Native American buying back Manhattan Island for $23.98 only to find it worth a mere $19.95; without the consent of the rock and roll audience, a Top 40 that is 70% rhythm and blues became no Top 40 at all!

R&B Influence Alternative Sound

For the purveyors of today's jangly rock and roll, having tired of waiting out the 90s in the vain hopes of regaining their previous lock on the demographic, simply decided, like a rich kid at a basketball court, to take their Spaldings to another court—a court where everyone is under six feet tall and can't jump. In this new court, variously known throughout the years as Punk, New Wave, Modern and PostModern Rock, today's Alternative sounds comprised an alternative mainstream that had all the self-righteous earmarks and over-adrenalized attitude of R&B-based rockabilly storming the barricades of pop in 1954. Plus, it had a good beat and you could identify with it.

Back then, most black music was portrayed as savage and simplistic, carnal and dangerous—even that most hallowed and reverential form of innocent romance we now know as doo-wop. Similarly, through the 90s, with Gangsta Rap taking most of the heat and the political bullets, the ominous tones from the boom boxes across the way represented what seemed to many like a shattering of the common bond between discourse and dischord, all harmony gone, all romance reduced to its most basic and base essentials. Threatening, yes, historically resonant, perhaps purposely hard to take, it contained all the elements necessary for good rock and roll, except a redeeming conscience, and maybe a bit of softening melody. Most of the black-owned Top 40 of 1995, however, contained far more innocuous pop and teen dance fodder than anything likely to cause a major label to cave, Congress to conspire, or candidates to dance in the street like dispossessed Vandelas.

In fact, the strongest comment of the year was Coolio's steadfastly anti-Gangsta "Gangsta's Paradise," taking up where Seal and Domino left off with "Prayer for the Dying" and "Gangsta Lean," respectively. While Gangsta Rap's reigning real-life gangsta types, Snoop Doggy Dogg and Tupak Shakur, both added hit records to their criminal records, with "Murder Was the Case" and "Dear Mama," respectively, by far the mainstream's prevailing flava was provided by Skee-Lo's captivating ditty "I Wish," this year's version of Ahmad's "Back in the Day," but hardly on the upward positive mobility scale of Des'ree's ubiquitous "You Gotta Be" from late '94.

Symbolizing the drift of the black Top 40 toward the kind of pop vapidity rock and roll has been historically mandated to destroy, Whitney Houston ("Waiting to Exhale"), Mariah Carey with Boyz II Men ("Fantasy," "One Sweet Day"), All-4-One ("I Can Love You Like That"), Babyface as the new Burt Bacharach (Jon B.'s "Pretty Girl," Madonna's "Take a Bow," "Water Runs Dry" by Boyz II Men, the whole *Waiting to Exhale* soundtrack), Seal (the multi-Grammy winning "Kiss from a Rose"), even the (black-led) so-called alternative feel-good bar band of the year, Hootie & the Blowfish ("Let Her Cry," "Hold My Hand"), all advanced toward some homogenized safe mean that probably threatened the sound as well as the relevance of Top 40 even more than rock music did in 1995.

Women Get Their Point Across

While African Americans were too entrenched or intoxicated by the trappings of their new power at the helm of rock and roll to effectively further a revolution, a similarly historically disenfranchised group came charging up the corridors this year to wrest away the mantle of relevance. If the year's assault on the R&B mainstream can be likened to the son rising up to smite the father, then this revolution resembled nothing so much as the daughter rising up to smite not only the father, but the brother as well. Angry young women like Polly Jean Harvey and Liz Phair, taking up where Courtney Love left off, echoed mythic forebears, from Sonic Youth's Kim Gordon to neo-beat poet Patti Smith, to the infinitely more genteel but no less irked Joni Mitchell. Alanis Morissette ("You Oughta Know"), the made-for-MTV equivalent of a rock and roll Glenn Close in *Fatal Attraction,* if ever there was one, was their symbolic, if overly slick, leader. But other ends of the anger spectrum were mined as well, from the previously meek Lisa Loeb ("Do You Sleep") to the righteously folkie Indigo Girls ("Bury My Heart at Wounded Knee").

On the notoriously acquiescent country music front, Shania Twain ("Any Man of Mine") and Lorrie Morgan ("I Didn't Know My Own Strength") made positive role model news. TLC's cautionary "Waterfalls" joined hands with Salt-N-Pepa's anthemic "Ain't Nothing but a She Thing," over in the R&B camps, while Dionne Ferris's plaintive "I Know" echoed Toni Braxton's subtle strength. Even Annie Lennox's pop foray ("No More I Love You's") had a feminist tone that would have had Helen Reddy smiling down from Las Vegas. Back in rock, the ladies of Garbage ("Vow," "Queer") and the Cranberries ("Zombie," "Ridiculous Thoughts") did Belly and the Bangles proud. The scorching Babes in Toyland covered Sister Sledge's "We Are Family," giving it a whole new rocking dimension. Jill Sobule offered the campy "I Kissed a Girl" into the mix. Björk earned more points for her unearthly presence with "Army of Me." Decidedly more earthy and profane, Joan Osborne ("St. Teresa," "One of Us") was the year's favorite singer/songwriter. Critic's darling P. J. Harvey ("Long Snake Moan," "Down by the Water") was, some said, the bluesiest raver since Robert Plant.

The British (Re)Invasion

Beyond Harvey, nearly anything British was suddenly more fashionable than it had been in at least ten, if not thirty, years. With the release of several volumes of Beatles arcana, including the re-constituted "Free as a Bird," second- and third-generation Beatlephiles were in abundance. Maybe the most historically devastating track to emerge this year from England was Sponge's "Molly," containing the resonant phrase: "Sixteen candles down the drain." You would have thought a group called Dead Beatles could have caught on after that. Instead, the classically Beatlesque "Wonderwall" by Oasis got all the play, effectively leaving the resurrected Beatles for dead. The Rolling Stones creaked and cranked their way through another tour, finally issuing their version of Bob Dylan's "Like a Rolling Stone," for the enlightenment of the young and the nostalgia of the old. The leaders of Led Zeppelin, Jimmy Page and Robert Plant, added to their platinum bank account with a reunion tour as well. But the new invasion was hardly about the Beatles and The Stones or even (thank God) Led Zeppelin. The Kinksian tones of Blur ("Country House"), Bush's velveteen "Glycerine," and the droning Stone Roses ("Love Spreads") were the primary colors. Radiohead ("Fake Plastic Trees") and Silverchair ("Pure Massacre") offered the intelligent pop of Squeeze and Prefab Sprout. Then there was Take That's undeniable "Back for Good," which briefly created a riotous fan response not seen in popdom since the heyday of the New Kids on the Block. And if you were looking to England as a source of the next underground, you might focus for a spell on Tricky, whose disco/techno/rapoid creations were causing the expected critical ripples.

Alternative Mainstream, Triple A, and Top 40 Don't Mix

Top 40 missed most of this action; instead it all took place in the new alternative mainstream, which finally started to take itself seriously in 1995, giving fans a notion of its history as well as its overabundant present. Thus, not only was Neil Young's collaboration with Eddie Vedder ("Downtown," "Peace and Love") exciting in its own right, it was an historically appropriate recognition of both rock and roll's contribution to today's alternative sound and its systematic absence from the Top 40 (an elimination process that started way back in the 70s). In this new historically aware genre, the Ramones ("I Don't Want to Grow Up") could get long-awaited airplay next to the Smashing Pumpkins ("Bullet with Butterfly Wings"). The Goo Goo Dolls ("Name") could be heard in context with their immediate forebears, the Replacements. Mike Watt ("Against the 70s" with Eddie Vedder) could also be heard in context with his legendary Minutemen. Yo Lo Tengo ("Tom Courtenay") and Morphine ("Honey White") could pay homage to Sonic Youth. Dave Grohl could resurrect the ghost of Nirvana with the Foo Fighters ("This Is a Call"). Neo jam bands Blues Traveler ("Run-Around") and the Dave Matthews Band ("What Would You Say") could resurrect the ghost of Jerry Garcia and the Grateful Dead (even before Jerry's sad passing, and even if "Run-Around" sounded more like a Springsteen song). The Presidents of the United States of America ("Lump") could bring back frat rock. Matthew Sweet ("Sick of Myself," "We're the Same") could put a twisted spin on the notion of the singer/songwriter. And Chrissie Hynde could be christened Godmother of Generation X ("Sense of Purpose"), even as she headlined the opening of the Rock and Roll Hall of Fame in her native city, Cleveland, and did a guest shot on the TV show *Friends* ("Angel of the Morning").

Todd Snider hilariously skewered that self-same age group in "My Genera-tion," one of the year's best Triple A (Adult Album Alternative) tunes. Just slightly to the left of the mainstream, the Triple A format claimed the edu-cated middle class portion of the mainstream alternative demographic. This is where educated, middle class folk/rock lived—under the rubric of Middle of the Dirt Road music. It was where you could hear the ethereal Alison Krauss singing "When You Say Nothing at All" on the tribute album to country singer Keith Whitley, and the still-ethereal Linda Ronstadt singing "Gainesville," the best thing on Randy Newman's rock operetta *Faust*. It was where Sonny Landreth's New Orleansiana ("South of I-10") bubbled and Little Feat's "Borderline Blues" cooked. Like those "over-30" golf and tennis circuits, where the legends play as well as ever among their own, the Triple A crowd welcomed the reformed Eagles back into the fold ("Get over It," "Love Will Keep Us Alive"). Brian Wilson was the subject of a poignant musical documentary, *I Just Wasn't Made for These Times,* and saw a long-awaited collaboration with Van Dyke Parks hit the street ("Orange Crate Art"). John Prine ("Lake Marie") was hailed as a returning deity. The newly-aged Natalie Merchant fit right in ("Carnival"). Jeff Buck-ley's aching tones reminded everyone of his late father Tim ("Last Good-bye"). Emmylou Harris delivered another prime album, even though it fea-tured songs by Lucinda Williams ("Sweet Old World"), Bob Dylan ("Every Grain of Sand") and Neil Young ("Wrecking Ball"). Bob Dylan himself played this circuit with "Dignity." Bruce Springsteen, once considered the next New Dylan ("Youngstown"), made his bid here to be the next Woody Guthrie. Tom Petty, who has long since retired the Best New Dylan title, continued his reign with "You Wreck Me" and "It's Good to Be King." Linda Ronstadt anointed Petty's old material with her legendary pipes ("The Waiting").

Even the best thing Broadway had to offer this year (if not the only new thing Broadway had to offer this year) was a Triple A coup: an entire evening's showcase of the great works of Leiber & Stoller, including some of their more obscure gems ("Some Cats Know" by Pattie Darcy Jones, "That Is Rock and Roll" by the entire company).

Tribute Albums Surge in Popularity

Even better than a cover tune, the tribute album continued to flourish in this sphere, enabling newer artists to finally have a chance to perform a good song, and rescuing superstars from the tyranny of always having to do only their own material. Lou Reed and Dion were among the more obvious types to celebrate songwriting legend Doc Pomus; Los Lobos did him proud with

"Lonely Avenue." Madonna and Massive Attack made an impact on the Marvin Gaye tribute album ("I Want You"). The Chieftains teamed with Sting on the second Leonard Cohen tribute album ("Sisters of Mercy"). A bunch of country singers celebrated the Beatles ("Nowhere Man" by Randy Travis, "Come Together" by Delbert McClinton). A horde of popsters celebrated Carole King's landmark *Tapestry* album, among them Amy Grant ("It's Too Late"), Rod Stewart ("So Far Away"), and Aretha Franklin with Bebe and Cece Winans ("You've Got a Friend"). Meanwhile, rock bands celebrated the work of Led Zeppelin ("Dancing Days" by Stone Temple Pilots)—as if the 80s hadn't been one long heavy metal tribute enough. More to Triple A liking, a spectacular cast was assembled to re-interpret one of the most popular musicals of all time, *West Side Story* ("America" by Natalie Cole, Patti LaBelle, and Sheila E., "Somewhere" by Phil Collins, "Tonight" by Kenny Loggins and Wynonna).

Movie Songs Have Big Year

Once again, many of the year's top Top 40 hits came from the only screen larger than MTV, the silver screen of the movies: "Kiss from a Rose," by Seal, from *Batman Forever,* "Gangsta's Paradise" by Coolio, from *Dangerous Minds,* the inevitable Bryan Adams' "Have You Ever Really Loved a Woman," from *Don Juan DeMarco,* the return of the Gin Blossoms with "Til I Hear It from You," from *Empire Records,* which also produced Edwin McCain's "A Girl Like You." The *Waiting to Exhale* soundtrack was greeted with at least as much if not more enthusiasm than the movie, and performed to a higher standard, with Whitney Houston's leadoff title track only the icing on the cake. Denied that kind of access to instant hit status, many other black artists needed the clout of the big screen to ensure record sales. From *Higher Learning* came "Ask of You" by Raphael Sadiq; from *New Jersey Drive* came "Can't You See" by Total, featuring the Notorious B.I.G. From *Panther,* came Joi's "The Pendulum Vibe"; from *The Show* came "How High" by Redman/Method Man; from *Tales from the Hood* came the title tune by Domino; from *Friday* came "Keep Their Heads Ringing" by Dr. Dre. "I Know" was originally featured in Robert Altman's *Ready to Wear.* ("Candy Rain" and "I Believe" by Soul for Real came from the TV soap opera *All My Children*).

Country Stays Conservative, Garth Catches a "Fever"

It was not all bad news on the Top 40 front, however. At least the format hadn't degenerated entirely into the kind of self-enclosed bedroom community that is country music. With its own Top 40 of endlessly recyclable material and sound-alike artists singing tailor-made songs, written five a day by the same forty songwriters—seemingly two-thirds of the hits reaching number one, and then disappearing overnight—the entrenched sound of country music has been a non-crossover world unto itself with only rare exception since Elvis left for Germany. And while the usual suspects like Alabama ("In Pictures"), John Michael Montgomery ("No Man's Land"), Reba McEntire ("The Heart Is a Lonely Hunter"), Patty Loveless ("You Don't Even Know My Name"), and especially Vince Gill ("Go Rest High on That Mountain") delivered wonderfully crafted and sometimes even heartfelt songs, the biggest news was made by one of the goodest of the good old boys, Garth Brooks, when he recruited a couple of bad old guys from the hard rock band Aerosmith to help co-write "The Fever." Would country music tolerate such outsiders? Especially from the ranks of the dreaded arch enemy rock and roll? Eventually, the furor subsided and the empire withstood the shocks. Alan Jackson jokingly summed up the country scene with "Gone Country." A better choice might have been Pam Tillis' "Mi Vida Loca (My Crazy Life)."

Non-Awards of the Year

Other than that small triumph, there were a only few sublime moments for the lifelong Top 40 fan—perhaps none quite as sublime as Mariah Carey's disgruntled expression at the Grammy Awards as she was shut out of all six trophies she was up for. There was Joan Osborne's nose ring. There was L.V., the secret hero of the Top 40, who sang the intense, impassioned hook on Coolio's "Gangsta's Paradise." The surprise interloper of the year was Lou Barlow, the low-fi underground outsider who achieved visibility with "Natural One," the Folk Implosion tune from the documentary *Kids*. You had Del Amitri's "Roll to Me," which would have sounded good in any of Top 40's several heydays ('57, '64, '84, to name just three). "Better Man" was Pearl Jam's best single yet, and they finally released "Yellow Ledbetter." Live continued its quest for the Truth in Rock title jointly held by U2 and REM with "Lightning Crashes," while REM ("Bang and Blame") and U2 ("Hold Me, Thrill Me, Kiss Me, Kill Me," "Miss Sarajevo"), showed no signs of giving it up. Rusted Root's "Send Me on My Way" was a left-field worldbeat smash out of, you guessed it, Pittsburgh. Title of the year belonged to alternative rockers Eve's Plum, with "Jesus Loves You, but Not as Much as I Do." Unfortunately, like most country tunes, the title was the best thing about it. Hook of the year was from "Good" by Better Than Ezra. Comeback of the year was Barry White ("Come On"). Go-Away of the Year award went to Michael Jackson ("Scream"). While the Song We Love to

Hate award was split between "I'll Be There for You" by the Rembrandts and "Breakfast at Tiffany's" by Deep Blue Something. What about the complete turnaround performed by Sophie B. Hawkins, who was last seen as an angry young woman herself, a couple of years ago, with "Damn, I Wish I Was Your Lover." This year her "As I Lay Me Down" was as calming and ethereal as Patience and Prudence at their best. Does this mean that next year we'll hear Fleetwood Mac covering the Fleetwoods or Alanis Morissette singing "I Am Woman" in Las Vegas? Without a viable Top 40 America would have to do without a definitive answer to these questions, which is reason enough to hope the plucky format does a turnaround itself.

Bruce Pollock

Editor

A

Adalita
Words and music by Mike Geiger, Woody Mullis, and Michael Huffman.
Sixteen Stars Music, 1994/Dixie Stars Music, 1994.
Best-selling record by George Strait from the album *Lead On* (MCA, 94).

After the Goldrush
Words and music by Neil Young.
Silver Fiddle, 1970.
Revived by Linda Ronstadt, Valerie Carter, and Emmylou Harris from the album *Feels Like Home* (Elektra, 95).

Against the 70s
Words and music by Mike Watt.
Thunderspiels Music, 1995.
Best-selling record by Mike Watt (featuring Eddie Vedder) from the album *Ball-Hog or Tugboat* (Columbia, 95).

Ain't Nothin' but a She Thing
Words and music by Cheryl James.
Bee Mo Easy, 1995.
Best-selling record by Salt-N-Pepa from the album *Ain't Nothin but a She Thing* (London, 95).

All Over You
Words and music by Edward Kowalcyzk, Patrick Dahlheimer, Chad Gracey, and Chad Taylor.
Loco De Amor, New York, 1994/Audible Sun, New York, 1994.
Best-selling record by Live from the album *Throwing Copper* (Radioactive/MCA, 94).

All That Heaven Will Allow
Words and music by Bruce Springsteen.
Bruce Springsteen Publishing, 1987.

Revived by The Mavericks from the album *What a Crying Shame* (MCA, 94).

Alright Guy
Words and music by Todd Snider.
Bro N' Sis Music, 1994/Keith Sykes Music, 1994.
Introduced by Todd Snider from the album *Songs for the Daily Planet* (MCA, 95).

America
Words and music by Stephen Sondheim and Leonard Bernstein.
Chappell & Co., Inc., 1957/Leonard Bernstein Music, 1957.
Revived by Natalie Cole, Patti LaBelle, and Sheila E. from the album *The Songs of West Side Story* (RCA, 95).

Amy's Back in Austin
Words and music by Brady Seals and Steven Davis.
Square West, 1994/Red Brazos, 1994/Howlin' Hits Music, 1994/Original Hometown Street Music, 1994.
Best-selling record by Little Texas from the album *Kick a Little* (Warner Brothers, 94).

And Fools Shine On
Words and music by Marti Fredrickson and Damon Johnson.
EMI-Virgin, 1995/Heathalee, 1995/Little Miss Music, 1995/EMI-Virgin Songs, 1995/Pearl White, 1995.
Best-selling record by Brother Cane from the album *Seeds* (Virgin, 95).

And Still
Words and music by Liz Hengler and Tommy Lee James.
Starstruck Writers Group, 1994/Starstruck Angel, 1995.
Best-selling record by Reba McEntire from the album *Read My Mind* (MCA, 94).

Angel of the Morning
Words and music by Chip Taylor.
EMI-Blackwood Music Inc., 1967.
Revived by The Pretenders from the album and TV soundtrack *Friends* (Reprise, 95).

Ants Marching
Words and music by Dave Matthews.
Colden Grey Music, New York, 1994.
Best-selling record by The Dave Matthews Band from the album *Under the Table and Dreaming* (RCA, 94).

Any Man of Mine
Words and music by Shania Twain and Robert John "Mutt" Lange.
Loon Echo Music, 1995/Zomba Music, 1995.

2

Best-selling record by Shania Twain from the album *The Woman in Me* (Mercury Nashville, 95). Nominated for a Grammy Award, Best Country Song of the Year, 1995.

Anything
Words and music by Taryll Jackson, T. J. Jackson, Taj Jackson, Alfons Kettner, and Bobby Caldwell.
To the T Music, Sherman Oaks, 1995.
Best-selling record by 3T from the album *Brotherhood* (MJJ/550 Music).

Army of Me (Swedish)
English words and music by Bjork (pseudonym for Bjork Gudmundsdottir) and Graham Massey.
F.S. Ltd., England, 1995/SPZ, 1995/Peermusic Ltd., 1995.
Best-selling record by Bjork from the album *Post* (Elektra, 95).

As Any Fool Can See
Words and music by Pete Nelson and Ken Beard.
Sony Tree Publishing, 1994/Terilee Music, 1994/New Clarion, 1994/Golden Reed, 1994.
Best-selling record by Tracy Lawrence from the album *I See It Now* (Atlantic, 94).

As I Lay Me Down
Words and music by Sophie B. Hawkins.
Night Rainbow Music, 1995/Broken Plate Music Inc., 1995.
Best-selling record by Sophie B. Hawkins from the album *Whaler* (Columbia, 95).

Ask of You
Words and music by Raphael Sadiq, Teddy Riley, Hachidai Nakamura, and Rokusuke Ei.
Toshiba Music Publishing Co., Ltd., Tokyo, Japan, 1995/Polygram International, 1995/Tony! Toni! Tone!, 1995/Regent Music, 1995.
Best-selling record by Raphael Sadiq from the film and soundtrack album *Higher Learning* (Epic Soundtrax, 95).

Atomic
Words and music by Deborah Harry and Chris Stein.
Monster Island, 1979/Chrysalis Music Group, 1979.
Revived by Blondie on the album *The Remix Project* (Chrysalis/EMI, 95).

Awake
Words and music by Letters to Cleo.
Warner-Tamerlane Music, 1995/Itchy Putschy, 1995.
Best-selling record by Letters to Cleo from the album *Wholesale Meat and Fish* (Giant, 95).

B

Baby
Words and music by Kevin Crouch, Kipper Jones, and Rahsaan
  Peterson.
Human Rhythm, 1994/Ecstasoul Music, 1994/Young Legend, 1994.
Best-selling record by Brandy from the album *Brandy* (Atlantic, 94).

Baby It's You
Words and music by Burt Bacharach, Mack David, and Barney
  Williams.
New Hidden Valley Music Co., 1961/EMI U Catalogue, 1961/Polygram
  International, 1961.
Revived by The Beatles on the album *Live at the BBC* (Capitol, 95),
  featuring previously unreleased live performances from early in their
  career.

Baby Now That I've Found You (English)
Words and music by John McLeod and Tony MacCaulay.
BMG Music, 1967.
Revived by Alison Krauss & Union Station on the album *Now That I
  Found You* (Rounder, 95).

Back for Good (English)
Words and music by Gary Barlow.
EMI-Virgin, 1995.
Best-selling record by Take That from the album *Back for Good* (Arista,
  95).

Back in Your Arms Again
Words and music by Fred Knoblock and Paul David.
Almo Music Corp., 1995/Garlicky Music, 1995/Paul & Jonathan Songs,
  1995/EMI-Virgin, 1995.
Best-selling record by Lorrie Morgan from the album *Greatest Hits*
  (BNA, 95).

Ballad of Peter Pumpkinhead (English)
Words and music by Andy Partridge.
Virgin Songs, 1992.
Revived by Crash Test Dummies in the film and on the soundtrack
album *Dumb and Dumber* (RCA, 95). This was an old XTC hit.

Bang and Blame
Words and music by Bill Berry, Peter Buck, Mike Mills, and Michael
Stipe.
Night Garden Music, 1994/Warner-Tamerlane Music, 1994.
Best-selling record by R.E.M. from the album *Monster* (Warner
Brothers, 95).

Be My Lover (German)
English words and music by G. Saraf, A. Brenner, M. Thornton, and L.
McCray.
FMP Music, 1995/Edition Beam Music, 1995/Warner-Chappell Music,
1995.
Best-selling record by La Bouche from the album *Sweet Dreams* (RCA,
95).

Beautiful Life (Swedish)
English words and music by J. Berggren and John Ballard.
Mega Music, 1995/Careers-BMG, 1995.
Best-selling record by Ace of Base from the album *The Bridge* (Arista,
95).

Before You Walk Out of My Life
Words and music by Andrea Martin, Carsten Schack, and Kenneth
Karlin.
Irving Music Inc., 1995/Casadida, 1995/EMI-Blackwood Music Inc.,
1995.
Best-selling record by Monica from the album *Miss Thang* (Arista, 95).

Believe (English)
Words and music by Elton John and Bernie Taupin.
William A. Bong Music, 1995/Harnia Music, 1995/WB Music, 1995.
Best-selling record by Elton John from the album *Made in England*
(Rocket/Island, 95).

Bend It until It Breaks
Words and music by John Anderson and Lionel Delmore.
Almo Music Corp., 1994/Holmes Creek Music, 1994/Polygram
International, 1994/Foggy Jonz Music, 1994.
Best-selling record by John Anderson from the album *Country Till I Die*
(BNA, 94).

Best Friend
Words and music by Kevin Crouch and Glenn McKinney.

Human Rhythm, 1994.
Best-selling record by Brandy from the album *Brandy* (Atlantic, 94).

Better Man
Words and music by Eddie Vedder, Dave Abbruzzese, Jeff Ament, Mike
    McCready, and Stone Gossard.
Honest Music, 1994/Scribing C-Ment Music, 1994/Write Treatage
    Music, 1994/Polygram International, 1994.
Best-selling record by Pearl Jam from the album *Vitalogy* (Epic, 94).

Better Than Nothing
Words and music by Jennifer Trynin.
Now Sam I Am Music, 1994.
Introduced by Jennifer Trynin on the album *Cockamamie* (Squint/
    Warner Brothers, 95).

Better Things to Do
Words and music by Tom Shapiro and Chris Waters.
Diamond Struck Music, 1995/Sony Tree Publishing, 1995/Great
    Cumberland Music, 1995/Tom Shapiro Music, 1995/Mike Curb
    Productions, 1995.
Best-selling record by Terri Clark from the album *Terri Clark* (Mercury
    Nashville, 95).

Big Poppa
Words and music by The Notorious B.I.G.
Tee Tee, 1995/Justin Publishing Co., 1995.
Best-selling record by The Notorious B.I.G. from the album *Ready to
    Die* (Bad Boy/Arista, 95).

Big Yellow Taxi
Words and music by Joni Mitchell.
Siquomb Publishing Corp., 1970.
Revived by Amy Grant on her album *House of Love* (A & M, 95) and
    by Joni Mitchell on her album *Friends*.

Bittersweetheart
Words and music by Dave Pirner.
LFR Music, 1995/WB Music, 1995.
Introduced by Soul Asylum on the album *Let Your Dim Light Shine*
    (Columbia, 95).

Blessed (English)
Words and music by Elton John and Bernie Taupin.
William A. Bong Music, 1995/Harnia Music, 1995/WB Music, 1995.
Best-selling record by Elton John from the album *Made in England*
    (Rocket/Island, 95).

Blind Man
Words and music by Steven Tyler, Joe Perry, and Taylor Rhodes.
Swag Song Music, 1994/EMI-April Music, 1995/Taylor Rhodes Music,
  1995/MCA Music, 1995.
Best-selling record by Aerosmith from the album *Big Ones* (Geffen, 94).

Blood Brothers
Words and music by Bruce Springsteen.
Bruce Springsteen Publishing, 1995.
Introduced by Bruce Springsteen on the album *Greatest Hits* (Columbia,
  95).

Blue
Words and music by Joni Mitchell.
Joni Mitchell Publishing Corp., 1995.
Revived by Sarah McLachlan on the album *Spirit of '73: Rock for
  Choice* (Epic, 95).

Boombastic
Words and music by Orville Burrell, King Floyd, and Robert
  Livingston.
Livingsting Music, 1995/Malaco Music Co., 1995.
Best-selling record by Shaggy from the album *Boombastic* (Virgin, 95).

Borderline Blues
Words and music by Billy Payne, Bill Wray, Paul Barrere, Shaun
  Murphy, and Fred Tackett.
Feat Music, 1995/Bill Wray Music, 1995/Polygram International, 1995.
Best-selling record by Little Feat from the album *Ain't Had Enough Fun*
  (Zoo, 95).

A Boy Like That
Words and music by Stephen Sondheim and Leonard Bernstein.
Chappell & Co., Inc., 1957/Leonard Bernstein Music, 1957.
Revived by Selena on the album *The Songs of West Side Story* (RCA,
  95).

Breakfast at Tiffanys
Words and music by Todd Pipes.
Deep Blue Something Music, 1995.
Best-selling record by Deep Blue Something from the album *Home*
  (Interscope/Atlantic, 95).

Bridge
Words and music by Chris DeGarmo.
Melodisc Music (ENGLAND), 1995.
Best-selling record by Queensryche from the album *Promised Land*
  (EMI, 95).

Broken Hearted
Words and music by Kevin Crouch and Kipper Jones.
Human Rhythm, 1994/Young Legend, 1994.
Best-selling record by Brandy from the album *Brandy* (Atlantic, 94).

Brown Sugar
Words and music by D'Angelo.
Ah Choo, 1995/Polygram International, 1995/12 AM, 1995/Jazz
  Merchant Music, 1995.
Best-selling record by D'Angelo from the album *Brown Sugar* (EMI,
  95). Nominated for a Grammy Award, Best R&B Song of the Year,
  1995.

Bullet with Butterfly Wings
Words and music by Billy Corgan.
South Mountain Music Corp., 1995/Cinderful, 1995.
Best-selling record by Smashing Pumpkins from the album *Mellon
  Collie & the Infinite Sadness* (Virgin, 95).

Bury My Heart at Wounded Knee
Words and music by Buffy Sainte-Marie.
Caleb Music, 1967/Almo Music Corp., 1967.
Revived by The Indigo Girls on the album *1200 Curfews* (Epic, 95).

C

Can I Touch You There
Words and music by Michael Bolton and Robert John "Mutt" Lange.
Warner-Chappell Music, 1995/Out of Pocket Music, 1995/Get Loose
    Music Inc., 1995/Zomba Music, 1995/Warner-Tamerlane Music,
    1995.
Best-selling record by Michael Bolton from the album *Michael Bolton--
    Greatest Hits, 1985--1995* (Columbia, 95).

Candy Rain
Words and music by Samuel Barnes, Terri Robinson, Jean Olivier, and
    Heavy D (pseudonym for Dwight Myers).
EZ Duz It, 1994/WB Music, 1994/Evelle Music, 1994/Twelve & Under,
    1994/Slam U Well Music, 1994.
Best-selling record by Soul for Real from the album *Candy Rain*
    (Uptown/MCA, 94).

Can't Cry Anymore
Words and music by Sheryl Crow.
Old Crow, Los Angeles, 1994/Ignorant, 1994/Warner-Tamerlane Music,
    1994.
Best-selling record by Sheryl Crow from the album *Tuesday Night
    Music Club* (A & M, 94).

Can't Really Be Gone
Words and music by Gary Burr.
MCA Music, 1995/Gary Burr Music, 1995.
Best-selling record by Tim McGraw from the album *All I Want* (Curb,
    95).

Can't Stop Loving You
Words and music by Eddie Van Halen, Alex Van Halen, Sammy Hagar,
    and Michael Anthony.
Yessup Music Co., 1995/WB Music, 1995.
Introduced by Van Halen on the album *Balance* (Warner Brothers, 95).

Can't You See
Words and music by J. Robinson, M. South, J. Howell, B. Ryan, Fred Wesley, John Starks, and Sean Combs.
Evelle Music, 1995/WB Music, 1995/South of Soul Music, 1995/EMI-Blackwood Music Inc., 1995/Big Herb Music, 1995/Janice Combs, 1995/12 AM, 1995/Late Hours Music, 1995.
Best-selling record by Total, featuring The Notorious B.I.G., in the film and on the soundtrack album *New Jersey Drive* (Tommy Boy, 95).

The Car
Words and music by Michael Spriggs and Gary Haydes.
Diamond Storm Music, 1995/EMI Tower Music, 1995/EMI-Blackwood Music Inc., 1995/Mike Curb Productions, 1995.
Best-selling record by Jeff Carson from the album *Jeff Carson* (Asylum, 95).

Carnival
Words and music by Natalie Merchant.
Indian Love Bride Music, New York, 1995.
Best-selling record by Natalie Merchant from the album *Tigerlily* (Elektra, 95).

Cell Therapy
Words and music by Robert Barnett, Thomas Burton, Cameron Gipp, and Willie Knighton, words and music by Organized Noize.
Organized Noize Music, Atlanta, 1995/Stiff Shirt, 1995/Goodie Mob Music, 1995.
Best-selling record by Cell Therapy from the album *Soul Food* (LaFace/Arista, 95).

Cemetery Gates
Words and music by Pantera.
Cota Music, 1995.
Introduced by Pantera from the film and soundtrack album *Demon Knight* (Atlantic, 95).

Check Yes or No
Words and music by Danny Wells and Dana Hunt Ogelsby.
John Juan, 1995/Victoria Kay Music, 1995.
Best-selling record by George Strait from the album *Strait out of the Box* (MCA, 95).

Childhood
Words and music by Michael Jackson.
Mijac Music, 1995/Warner-Tamerlane Music, 1995.
Introduced by Michael Jackson on the album *HIStory* (Epic, 95).

Colors of the Wind
Words and music by Alan Menken and Stephen Schwartz.

Wonderland Music, 1995/Walt Disney Music, 1995.
Best-selling record by Vanessa Williams from the film and soundtrack
   album *Pocahontas* (Hollywood, 95). Won an Academy Award for
   Best Song of the Year 1995;a Grammy Award for Best Song for TV
   or Movie 1995.

Come and Get Your Love
Words and music by Lolly Vegas.
EMI-Blackwood Music Inc., 1973/Novalene Music, 1973.
Revived by Real McCoy on the album *Another Night* (Arista, 94).

Come On
Words and music by James Harris, III, Terry Lewis, Barry White, and
   James Wright.
Flyte Tyme Tunes, 1995/New Perspective Publishing, Inc., 1995/Seven,
   1995/Super, 1995.
Best-selling record by Barry White from the album *The Icon Is Love* (A
   & M, 95).

Come Together
Words and music by John Lennon and Paul McCartney.
Northern Songs, Ltd., England, 1969/ATV Music Corp., 1969/EMI-
   Blackwood Music Inc., 1969.
Revived by Delbert McClinton on the album *Come Together: America
   Salutes The Beatles* (Liberty, 95) and Michael Jackson on the album
   HIStory (Epic, 95).

Comedown (English)
Words and music by Gavin Rossdale.
Warner-Tamerlane Music, 1995/Mad Dog Winston Music, 1995/Truly
   Soothing Elevator Music, 1995.
Best-selling record by Bush from the album *Sixteen Stone* (Trauma/
   Interscope, 95).

Connection
Words and music by Justine Frischman, words and music by Elastica.
EMI-Blackwood Music Inc., 1995.
Best-selling record by Elastica from the album *Elastica* (Geffen, 95).

Cool
Words and music by Stephen Sondheim and Leonard Bernstein.
Chappell & Co., Inc., 1957/Leonard Bernstein Music, 1957.
Revived by Patti Austin, Mervyn Warren, and Bruce Hornsby on the
   album *The Songs of West Side Story* (RCA, 95).

Corduroy
Words and music by Pearl Jam.
Honest Music, 1994/Write Treatage Music, 1994/Jumping Cat Music,

13

1994/Scribing C-Ment Music, 1994/Pickled Fish Music, 1994.
Best-selling record by Pearl Jam from the album *Vitalogy* (Epic, 95).

Cotton Eyed Joe
Words and music by Jan Ericcsson, Pat Reiniz, and Oban.
Zomba Music, 1995.
Best-selling record by Rednex from the album *Sex and Violins* (Battery/
Jive, 95).

Country House (English)
Words and music by Damon Albarn, Graham Coxon, Alex James, and
Dave Roundtree.
Music Corp. of America, 1995.
Best-selling record by Blur from the album *The Great Escape* (Food/
Virgin, 95).

Crash (English)
Words and music by Paul Court.
Complete Music (England), 1989.
Revived by The Primitives in the film and on the soundtrack album
Dumb and Dumber (RCA, 95).

Crazy Cool
Words and music by Peter Lord, Sandra St. Victor, and V. Jeffrey
Smith.
Leo Sun Music, 1995/Arvemal Music, 1995/Maanami Music, 1995/EMI-
April Music, 1995.
Introduced by Paula Abdul on the album *Head over Heels* (Virgin, 95).

Crazy World (American-English)
Words and music by Leslie Briccusse and Henry Mancini.
Stage & Screen Music Inc., 1981/EMI Variety Catalogue, 1981.
Revived by Julie Andrews in the musical *Victor/Victoria*.

Creep
Words and music by Dallas Austin.
ATV Music Corp., 1994/D.A.R.P. Music, 1994.
Best-selling record by TLC from the album *Crazysexycool* (LaFace, 94).
Nominated for a Grammy Award, Best R&B Song of the Year, 1995.

Crush with Eyeliner
Words and music by Bill Berry, Peter Buck, Mike Mills, and Michael
Stipe.
Warner-Tamerlane Music, 1994/Night Garden Music, 1994.
Best-selling record by R.E.M. from the album *Monster* (Warner
Brothers, 94).

Crusin'
Words and music by Smokey Robinson and Marv Tarplin.

14

Bertam Music Co., 1984.
Revived by D'Angelo on the album *Brown Sugar* (EMI, 95).

Cumbersome
Words and music by John Pollock and John Ross.
Crimson Music, 1995/EMI-Blackwood Music Inc., 1995.
Best-selling record by Seven Mary Three from the album *American Standard* (Mammoth/Atlantic, 95).

D

Dancing Days (English)
Words and music by Jimmy Page and Robert Plant.
Superhype Publishing, 1973.
Revived by Stone Temple Pilots on the album *Encomium: A Tribute to Led Zeppelin* (Atlantic, 95).

Darned If I Don't (Danged If I Do)
Words and music by Ronnie Dunn and Dean Dillon.
Sony Music, 1995/Acuff Rose Music, 1995.
Best-selling record by Shenandoah from the album *Somewhere in the Vicinity of the Heart* (Capitol Nashville, 95).

Days Like This (English)
Words and music by Van Morrison.
Exile Music, Memphis, 1995.
Introduced by Van Morrison on the album *Days Like This* (Polydor, 95).

Dead Man Walking
Words and music by Bruce Springsteen.
Bruce Springsteen Publishing, 1995.
Introduced by Bruce Springsteen in the film and on the soundtrack album *Music Inspired by the Film Dead Man Walking* (Columbia, 96). Nominated for an Academy Award, Best Song of the Year, 1995.

Dear Mama
Words and music by Tupac Shakur and Tony Pizzaro.
Joshua's Dream Music, 1995/Interscope Pearl, 1995/Warner-Tamerlane Music, 1995/Underground Connection Music, 1995.
Best-selling record by 2Pac from the album *Me Against the World* (Interscope, 95).

December
Words and music by Ed Roland.
Roland/Lentz, New York, 1995/Warner-Chappell Music, 1995.

Best-selling record by Collective Soul from the album *Collective Soul* (Atlantic, 95).

Deep as You Go
Words and music by Julie Flanders and Emil Adler.
F.S. Ltd., England, 1995/October Project, 1995.
Introduced by October Project on the album *Falling Farther In* (Epic, 95).

Diggin' on You
Words and music by Babyface (pseudonym for Kenny Edmunds).
Ecaf, 1994/Sony Music, 1994.
Best-selling record by TLC from the album *Crazysexycool* (LaFace, 94).

Dignity
Words and music by Bob Dylan.
Special Rider Music, 1994.
Introduced by Bob Dylan on the album *Greatest Hits III* (Columbia, 94). Nominated for a Grammy Award, Best Rock Song of the Year, 1995.

Dinosaur (English)
Words and music by Adrian Belew, words and music by King Crimson.
Crimson Music, 1995/BMG Music, 1995.
Introduced by King Crimson from the album *Thrak* (Virgin, 95).

Do You Sleep
Words and music by Lisa Loeb.
Furious Rose, New York, 1995.
Best-selling record by Lisa Loeb & Nine Stories from the album *Tails* (Geffen, 95).

Doctor Time
Words and music by Susan Longacre and William Wilson.
WB Music, 1994/Long Acre Music, 1994/Zomba Music, 1994.
Best-selling record by Rick Trevino from the album *Rick Trevino* (Columbia, 94).

Don't Ever Touch Me (Again)
Words and music by Dionne Farris and David Harris.
Peace Pourage Music, 1995/Dionne Yvette, 1995/Sony Songs, 1995.
Best-selling record by Dionne Farris from the album *Wild Seed--Wild Flower* (Columbia, 95).

Don't Take It Personal
Words and music by Dallas Austin and Derrick Simmons.
D.A.R.P. Music, 1995/Afro Dredite Music, 1995/Nu Rhythm & Life Music, 1995.

Best-selling record by Monica from the album *Miss Thang* (Rowdy/ Arista, 95).

Don't Tell Me (What Love Can Do)
Words and music by Eddie Van Halen, Alex Van Halen, Sammy Hagar, and Michael Anthony.
Yessup Music Co., 1994.
Best-selling record by Van Halen from the album *Balance* (Warner Brothers, 94).

Down by the Water
Words and music by Polly Jean Harvey.
Hot Head Ltd. (England), 1995.
Introduced by P. J. Harvey on the album *To Bring You My Love* (Island, 95).

Downtown
Words and music by Neil Young.
Silver Fiddle, 1995.
Introduced by Neil Young on the album *Mirror Ball* (Reprise, 95).
   Nominated for a Grammy Award, Best Rock Song of the Year, 1995.

Downtown Venus
Words and music by Atrel Cordes and Joe South.
MCA Music, 1995/Lowery Music Co., Inc., 1995.
Best-selling record by P.M. Dawn from the album *Jesus Wept* (Gee Street/Island, 95).

Dream about You
Words and music by Tolga Katas, Frank D'Allesandro, and Stevie B.
B and It Is Music, 1995/Turkishman, 1995.
Best-selling record by Stevie B. from the album *Funky Melody* (Emporia West/Thump, 95).

Dreaming of You
Words and music by Franne Golde and Tom Snow.
EMI-Virgin, 1995/Chesca Music, 1995/Snow Music, 1995.
Best-selling record by Selena from the album *Dreaming of You* (EMI Latin, 95).

Dust on the Bottle
Words and music by David Lee Murphy.
N2D Publishing, 1995.
Best-selling record by David Lee Murphy from the album *Out with a Bang* (MCA, 94).

E

Everlasting Love
Words and music by Buzz Cason and Mack Gaydon.
EMI-Blackwood Music Inc., 1974/Rising Sons Music, Inc., 1974.
Revived by Gloria Estefan on the album *Hold Me, Thrill Me, Kiss Me*
    (Epic, 94).

Every Grain of Sand
Words and music by Bob Dylan.
Special Rider Music, 1984.
Revived by Emmylou Harris on the album *Wrecking Ball* (Asylum, 95).

Every Little Thing I Do
Words and music by Heavy D (pseudonym for Dwight Myers), Terri
    Robinson, Jean Olivier, and Samuel Barnes.
EMI-April Music, 1994/Soul on Soul Music, 1994/WB Music, 1994/
    Evelle Music, 1994/Twelve & Under, 1994/Slam U Well Music,
    1994/Taking Care of Business Music, 1994.
Best-selling record by Soul for Real from the album *Candy Rain*
    (Uptown/MCA, 94).

Everyday Is Like Sunday
Words and music by Stephen Morrissey and Stephen Street.
Linder Ltd., 1988/WB Music, 1988/SBS Productions, 1988.
Revived by The Pretenders in the film and on the soundtrack album
    Boys on the Side (Arista, 95).

Everything Zen (English)
Words and music by Gavin Rossdale.
Mad Dog Winston Music, 1994.
Best-selling record by Bush from the album *Everything Zen* (Trauma/
    Interscope, 95).

Everytime You Touch Me
Words and music by Moby.
Warner-Tamerlane Music, 1995/Little Pitt Music, 1995.

21

Best-selling record by Moby from the album *Everything is Wrong* (Elektra, 95).

Exhale (Shoop Shoop)
Words and music by Babyface (pseudonym for Kenny Edmunds).
Ecaf, 1995/Sony Music, 1995/Fox Film Music Corp., 1995.
Best-selling record by Whitney Houston from the film and soundtrack album *Waiting to Exhale* (Arista, 95).

F

Fake Plastic Trees (English)
Words and music by Radiohead.
Warner-Chappell Music, 1995.
Best-selling record by Radiohead from the album *Fake Plastic Trees*
  (Capitol, 95).

Fantasy
Words and music by Mariah Carey, Dave Hall, Adrian Belew, Steven
  Stanley, Chris Franz, and Tina Weymouth.
Rye Songs, 1995/Metered Music, Inc., 1995/Polygram Music Publishing
  Inc., 1995/Sony Music, 1995/Stone Jam Music, 1995/Ness, Nitty &
  Capone, 1995.
Best-selling record by Mariah Carey from the album *Daydream*
  (Columbia, 95).

Feel Me Flow
Words and music by Keir Gist, Vincent Brown, Arthur Neville, Joseph
  Modeliste, Jr., Leo Nocentelli, and Leo Porter.
So So Def Music, 1995/EMI-April Music, 1995/Air Control, 1995.
Best-selling record by Naughty by Nature from the album *Poverty's
  Paradise* (Tommy Boy, 95).

Feels Like Home
Words and music by Randy Newman.
Randy Newman Music, 1995.
Introduced by Bonnie Raitt on the album *Randy Newman's Faust*
  (Warner Brothers, 95). Performed by Linda Ronstadt on the album
  Feels Like Home (Elektra, 95).

Feels So Good
Words and music by Jermaine Dupri and Carl Lowe, words and music
  by Xscape.
So So Def Music, 1995/EMI-April Music, 1995/Air Control, 1995.
Best-selling record by Xscape from the album *Off the Hook* (So So Def/
  Columbia, 95).

The Fever
Words and music by Dan Roberts, Steven Tyler, Joe Perry, and Bryan
   Kennedy.
Swag Song Music, 1995/EMI-April Music, 1995/Rope and Dally Music,
   1995/Old Boots Music, 1995.
Best-selling record by Garth Brooks from the album *Fresh Horses*
   (Capitol Nashville, 95).

First of the Month
Words and music by Bone, U-Neek, and Monte Powell.
Ruthless Attack Muzick, 1995/Dollarz N Sense Musick, 1995/Mo Thug
   Music, 1995/Keeno Music, 1995/Butter Jinx Music, 1995/Woodsongs,
   1995.
Best-selling record by Bone Thugs in Harmony from the album *E-1999
   Eternal* (Ruthless/Relativity, 95).

The First Step
Words and music by Doug Crider and Verlon Thompson.
Stroudacaster, 1994/Lazy Kato Music, 1994/EMI-April Music, 1994/Ides
   of March Music Division, 1994.
Best-selling record by Tracy Bird from the album *No Ordinary Man*
   (MCA, 94).

Foolin' Around
Words and music by Robert Kelly.
Zomba Music, 1994.
Best-selling record by Changing Faces from the album *Changing Faces*
   (Spoiled Rotten/Big Beat/Atlantic, 95).

For a Change
Words and music by Steve Seskin and John Scott Sherrill.
Love This Town, 1995/All Over Town, 1995/New Wolf, 1995/Tree
   Publishing Co., Inc., 1995.
Best-selling record by Neal McCoy from the album *You Gotta Love
   That* (Atlantic, 95).

For Your Love
Words and music by Stevie Wonder.
Steveland Music, Burbank, 1995.
Introduced by Stevie Wonder on the album *Conversation Piece*
   (Motown, 95). Won a Grammy Award for Best R&B Song of the
   Year 1995.

(It Won't Take) Forever Tonight
Words and music by Eric Carmen and Andy Goldmark.
New Nonpariel, 1995/WB Music, 1995/Eric Carmen, 1995/Polygram
   International, 1995.

Best-selling record by Peter Cetera and Crystal Bernard from the album *One Clear Voice* (River North, 95).

Forever Young
Words and music by Bob Dylan.
Special Rider Music, 1974.
Revived by Rebbie Jackson and The Pretenders in the film and soundtrack album *Free Willy 2--The Adventure Home* (MJJ/550 Music, 95).

Freak Like Me
Words and music by Eugene Hanes, Mark Valentine, Loren Hill, George Clinton, William Collins, and Gaylee Cooper.
Hanes, Hill & Valentine Music, 1995/Rubber Band, 1995/Polygram International, 1995.
Best-selling record by Adina Howard from the album *Do You Wanna Ride* (Mecca Don/East-West, 95).

Freak You
Words and music by DeVante.
Deswing Mob, 1995/EMI-April Music, 1995.
Best-selling record by Jodeci from the album *The Show, the After Party, the Hotel* (Uptown, 95).

Free as a Bird
Words and music by John Lennon, Paul McCartney, George Harrison, and Richard Starkey.
Lenono Music, 1977.
Best-selling record by The Beatles from the album *Anthology I* (Apple/Capitol, 95). Rare Lennon outtake resuscitated by the living Beatles to form the first new Beatle single in twenty years.

Free to Be
Words and music by RuPaul Charles and Jimmy Harry.
T-mo Music, 1995/Itself Music, 1995/RuPaul Charles Music, 1995/EMI-Virgin, 1995/Whonga Music, 1995.
Introduced by RuPaul in the film and on the soundtrack album *Wigstock* (Epic Soundtrax, 95).

Freedom
Words and music by Dallas Austin, J. Kirkland, and J. Gillman.
Butter Jinx Music, 1995/EMI-April Music, 1995/D.A.R.P. Music, 1995/Patrick Moxey Music, 1995/Enjoi Music, 1995/Diggin in the Crates Music, 1995.
Best-selling record by Vanessa Williams, TLC, Salt-N-Pepa, En Vogue, and Mary J. Blige from the film and soundtrack album *Panther* (Mercury, 95). Introduced by Joi on the album *The Pendulum Vibe* (Mercury, 95).

Friends of P
Words and music by Matt Sharp.
Powhatan Music, 1995.
Best-selling record by The Rentals from the album *Return of the Rentals* (Maverick/Reprise, 95).

G

Gainesville
Words and music by Randy Newman.
Randy Newman Music, 1995.
Introduced by Linda Ronstadt on the album *Randy Newman's Faust*
(Warner Brothers, 95).

Gangsta's Paradise
Words and music by Artis Ivey, Jr., Larry Sanders, Doug Rasheed, and
Stevie Wonder.
T-Boy Music Publishing Co., Inc., 1995/O/B/O/Itself, 1995/Larry
Sanders Music, 1995/Maria Belle, 1995/Mad Castle Music, 1995.
Best-selling record by Coolio from the film and soundtrack album
Dangerous Minds (MCA Soundtracks, 95). Nominated for a Grammy
Award, Record of the Year, 1995.

Geek Stink Breath
Words and music by Billy Joe Armstrong, words and music by Green
Day.
WB Music, 1995/Green Daze, 1995.
Best-selling record by Green Day from the album *Insomniac* (Reprise,
95).

Gel
Words and music by Ed Roland.
Roland/Lentz, New York, 1995.
Introduced by Collective Soul from the film and soundtrack album *The
Jerky Boys* (Atlantic, 95).

Get Down
Words and music by Craig Mack.
For Ya Ear, 1995/Justin Publishing Co., 1995/Bee Mo Easy, 1995/EMI-
April Music, 1995.
Best-selling record by Craig Mack from the album *Craig Mack* (Arista,
95).

Get over It
Words and music by Don Henley and Glenn Frey.
Red Cloud Music Co., 1994/Songs of All Nations Music, 1994/WB
  Music, 1994.
Best-selling record by The Eagles from the album *Hell Freezes Over*
  (Geffen, 95).

Get Ready for This
Words and music by Raymond Slegngaard, Felipe Wilde, and Jean Paul
  Decoster.
Any Kind of Music, 1995/MCA Music, 1995.
Best-selling record by 2Unlimited (Radikal/Critique, 94).

Get Together
Words and music by Chester Powers.
Irving Music Inc., 1965.
Revived by Big Mountain on the album *Resistance* (Giant, 95).

A Girl Like You
Words and music by Edwyn Collins.
Edwyn Collins Music, 1995.
Best-selling record by Edwyn Collins from the film and soundtrack
  album *Empire Records* (A & M, 95). Also featured on *Gorgeous
  George* (Bar None, 95).

Give It to You
Words and music by Jermaine Dupri and C. Kelly.
My World, Atlanta, 1995/So So Def Music, 1995/EMI-April Music,
  1995.
Best-selling record by Da Brat from the album *Funkdafied* (So So Def,
  95).

Give Me One More Shot
Words and music by Teddy Gentry, Randy Owen, and Ronnie Rogers.
Maypop Music, 1994/Wild Country Music, 1995.
Best-selling record by Alabama from the album *Greatest Hits, Volume
  III* (RCA, 94).

Glycerine (English)
Words and music by Gavin Rossdale.
Mad Dog Winston Music, 1995/Truly Socthing Elevator Music, 1995.
Best-selling record by Bush from the album *Sixteen Stone* (Trauma/
  Interscope, 95).

Go Rest High on That Mountain
Words and music by Vince Gill.
Benefit Music, 1994.
Best-selling record by Vince Gill on the album *When Love Finds You*

(MCA, 94). Won a Grammy Award for Best Country Song of the Year 1995.

Goin' through the Big D
Words and music by Ronnie Rogers, Jon Wright, and Mark Wright.
Maypop Music, 1994.
Best-selling record by Mark Chesnutt from the album *What a Way to Live* (Decca, 94).

Gold
Words and music by Prince (pseudonym for Prince Rogers Nelson).
Controversy Music, 1995.
Best-selling record by Prince from the album *The Gold Experience* (NPG/Warner Brothers, 95).

Goldeneye
Words and music by Bono (pseudonym for Paul Hewson) and Edge (pseudonym for Dave Evans).
Polygram International, 1995.
Introduced by Tina Turner in the film and on the soundtrack album *Goldeneye* (Virgin, 95).

Gone Country
Words and music by Bob McDill.
Polygram International, 1994/Ranger Bob Music, 1994.
Best-selling record Alan Jackson from the album *Who I Am* (Arista, 94). Nominated for a Grammy Award, Best Country Song of the Year, 1995.

Gonna Get a Life
Words and music by Frank Dycus and Jim Lauderdale.
Al Andersongs, Nashville, 1994/Warner Source Music, 1994/Dyinda Jams Music, 1994/Mighty Nice Music, 1994.
Best-selling record by Mark Chesnutt from the album *What a Way to Live* (Decca, 94).

Good
Words and music by Kevin Griffin.
Tentative Music, New Orleans, 1995.
Best-selling record by Better Than Ezra from the album *Deluxe* (Elektra, 95).

Good Intentions
Words and music by Glen Phillips and Toad the Wet Sprocket.
Wet Sprocket Songs, 1995/Sony Music, 1995.
Best-selling record by Toad the Wet Sprocket from the album and TV show soundtrack *Friends* (Reprise, 95).

H

Hakuna Matata (English)
Words and music by Tim Rice and Elton John.
Wonderland Music, 1995.
Best-selling record by Jimmy Cliff (featuring Lebo M.), from the film and soundtrack album *The Lion King* (Disney, 95).

Hand in My Pocket
Words and music by Glen Ballard and Alanis Morissette.
MCA Music, 1995/Van Hurst Place Music, 1995/Aerostation Corp., 1995.
Best-selling record by Alanis Morissette from the album *Jagged Little Pill* (Maverick/Reprise, 95).

Hard as a Rock (English)
Words and music by Angus Young and Malcolm Young.
Best-selling record by AC/DC from the album *Ballbreaker* (Atlantic, 95).

Have You Ever Really Loved a Woman
Words and music by Bryan Adams, Robert John "Mutt" Lange, and Michael Kamen.
Badams Music, 1995/Zomba Music, 1995/K-Man, 1995/New Line, 1995/Sony Songs, 1995.
Best-selling record by Bryan Adams from the film and soundtrack album *Don Juan DeMarco* (A&M, 95). Nominated for an Academy Award, Best Song of the Year, 1995; a Grammy Award, Best Song for TV or Movie, 1995.

Heart Is a Lonely Hunter
Words and music by Mark D. Sanders, Ed Hill, and Kim Williams.
Starstruck Writers Group, 1994/Mark D. Music, 1995/Sony Cross Keys Publishing Co. Inc., 1995/New Haven, 1995.
Best-selling record by Reba McEntire from the album *Read My Mind* (MCA, 94).

Here
Words and music by Gabrielle Glaser and Jill Cuniff.
EMI-April Music, 1995/Grand Royal Music, 1995/Luscious Jackson Music, 1995.
Introduced by Luscious Jackson in the film and on the soundtrack album *Clueless* (Grand Royal/East-West, 95).

Here and Now
Words and music by Letters to Cleo.
Rebecca Lilla Music, 1995/Famous Music Corp., 1995.
Introduced by Letters to Cleo on the album *Melrose Place* (Giant, 95).
Also on the album *Aurora Gory Alice* (Giant, 95).

Here I Am
Words and music by Tony Arata.
Morganactive Music, 1994/Pookie Bear, 1994.
Best-selling record by Patty Loveless from the album *When Fallen Angels Fly* (Epic, 94).

He's Mine
Words and music by Hamir, Mokenstef, Prince (pseudonym for Prince Rogers Nelson), and Roger Troutman.
All Init, 1995/Mo Thug Music, 1995/Hame Waje Music, 1995/ Controversy Music, 1995/WB Music, 1995/Songs of Castada, 1995/ Saja Music Co., 1995/Rubber Band, 1995.
Best-selling record by Mokenstef from the album *Azz Izz* (Outburst/ RAL/Island, 95).

Hey Lover
Words and music by Rod Temperton and LL Cool J.
Rodsongs, 1995/LL Cool J Music, 1995/Almo Music Corp., 1995.
Best-selling record by LL Cool J from the album *Mr. Smith* (Def Jam/ RAL/Island, 95).

Hey Man, Nice Shot
Words and music by Richard Patrick.
Buddy Doiwer Music, 1995.
Best-selling record by Filter from the album *Short Bus* (Reprise, 95).

Hey Now (Girls Just Want to Have Fun)
Words and music by Robert Hazard.
Sony Music, 1979.
Revived by Cyndi Lauper in the film and on the soundtrack album *To Wong Foo, Love Julie Newmar* (Epic Soundtrax, 95).

High Sierra
Words and music by H. L. Allen.
Coburn, 1995/Black Cypress Music, 1995.

Introduced by Linda Ronstadt on the album *Feels Like Home* (Elektra, 95).

Hold Me, Thrill Me, Kiss Me, Kill Me
Words and music by Bono (pseudonym for Paul Hewson), words and music by U2.
Polygram International, 1995.
Introduced by U2 in the film and on the soundtrack album *Original Music from the Motion Picture Batman Forever* (Island, 95).
Nominated for a Grammy Award, Best Rock Song of the Year, 1995.

Hold On (Canadian)
Words and music by Sarah McLachlan.
Sony Songs, 1995/Tyde, 1995.
Best-selling record by Sarah McLachlan from the album *Fumbling Toward Ecstacy* (Arista, 94).

Hold On
Words and music by Steve Tyrell, Kevin Savigar, Jamie Walters, and Stephanie Tyrell.
Tyrell Music Group, 1995/EMI-Blackwood Music Inc., 1995/Jamie Walters Music, 1995/Kevin Savigar, 1995/Almo Music Corp., 1995.
Best-selling record by Jamie Walters from the album *Jamie Walters* (Atlantic, 95).

Home Is Where the Heart Is
Words and music by Sally Fingeret.
Green Fingers Music, 1995.
Introduced by Peter, Paul & Mary on the album *Lifelines* (Warner Brothers, 95).

Honey White
Words and music by Mark Sandman.
Pubco Music, Ardmore, 1995/Head with Wings Music, 1995.
Best-selling record by Morphine from the album *Yes* (Rkyodisc, 95).

House of Love
Words and music by Walter Wilson, Kim Greenburg, and Greg Barnhill.
Sony Cross Keys Publishing Co. Inc., 1994/Greenburg Music, 1994/Tree Publishing Co., Inc., 1994/Warneractive Songs, 1994.
Best-selling record by Amy Grant and Vince Gill from the album *House of Love* (A & M, 94).

How High
Words and music by R. Noble, Erick Sermon, and C. Smith.
Full Volume Music, 1995/Careers-BMG, 1995/Wu-Tang Music, 1995/Zomba Music, 1995/Erick Sermon, 1995.
Best-selling record by Redman/Method Man from the film and soundtrack album *The Show* (Def Jam/RAL/Island, 95).

Hurricane
Words and music by Carlene Carter and Al Anderson.
High Steppe, Ventura, 1995/Al Andersongs, Nashville, 1995/Humble
　Artist, 1995/Mighty Nice Music, 1995.
Introduced by Carlene Carter from the album *Little Acts of Treason*
　(Giant/Warner Brothers, 95).

Hurt
Words and music by Trent Reznor.
Almo Music Corp., 1994.
Introduced by Nine Inch Nails on the album *Closer* (TVT, 94).
　Nominated for a Grammy Award, Best Rock Song of the Year, 1995.

I

I Believe
Words and music by Eliot Sloan, Jeff Pence, and Emosia.
EMI Songs Ltd., 1995/Tosha Music, 1995/Shapiro, Bernstein & Co., Inc., 1995.
Best-selling record by Blessid Union of Soul from the album *Home* (EMI, 95). It was introduced on the soap opera *All My Children*.

I Can Love You Like That
Words and music by Steve Diamond, Maribeth Derry, and Jennifer Kimball.
Diamond Cuts Music, 1995/Wonderland Music, 1995/Criterion Music Corp., 1995/Second Wave Music, 1995/Full Keel Music, 1995/Friends and Angels Music, 1995.
Best-selling record by John Michael Montgomery from the album *John Michael Montgomery* (Atlantic, 95). Nominated for Grammy Awards, Best Country Song of the Year, 1995 and Song of the Year, 1995.

I Can't Tell You Why
Words and music by Timothy Schmidt, Don Henley, and Glenn Frey.
Red Cloud Music Co., 1979/Jeddrah Music, 1979/Cass County Music Co., 1979.
Revived by Brownstone on the album *From the Bottom Up* (MJJ/Epic, 94).

I Could Fall in Love
Words and music by Keith Thomas.
Sony Music, 1995/Yellow Elephant Music, 1995.
Best-selling record by Selena from the album *Dreaming of You* (EMI Latin, 95).

I Didn't Know My Own Strength
Words and music by Rick Bowles and Robert Byrne.
Maypop Music, 1995/Nineteenth Hole Music, 1995/Bellarmine Music, 1995.

Best-selling record by Lorrie Morgan from the album *Greatest Hits* (BNA, 95).

I Don't Believe in Goodbyes
Words and music by Mark Miller, Scott Emerick, and Bryan White.
Traveling Zoo, 1995/Club Zoo Music, 1995/Seventh Son, 1995.
Best-selling record by Sawyer Brown from the album *Greatest Hits, 1990--1995* (Curb, 95).

I Don't Even Know Your Name
Words and music by Alan Jackson, Ron Jackson, and Andy Loftin.
WB Music, 1994.
Best-selling record by Alan Jackson from the album *Who Am I* (Arista, 94).

I Don't Want to Grow Up
Words and music by Tom Waits and Kathleen Brennan.
Jalma Music, 1992.
Revived by The Ramones on the album *Adios Amigos!* (Radioactive, 95).

I Feel Love
Words and music by Donna Summer, Giorgio Moroder, and Pete Bellotte.
Rick's Music Inc., 1977.
Revived by Blondie on the album *Remixed Remade Remodeled* (Chrysalis/EMI, 95).

I Feel Pretty
Words and music by Stephen Sondheim and Leonard Bernstein.
Chappell & Co., Inc., 1957/Leonard Bernstein Music, 1957.
Revived by Little Richard on the album *The Songs of West Side Story* (RCA, 95).

I Got a Girl
Words and music by Tim DeLaughter.
Chrysalis Songs, 1995/Pink Jelly Music, 1995.
Best-selling record by Tripping Daisy from the album *I Am an Elastic Firecracker* (Island, 95).

I Got 5 on It
Words and music by Garrick Husbands, Jerome Ellis, Anthony Gilmer, Jay King, Denzil Foster, and Thom McElroy, words and music by Kool & the Gang.
Stackola Music, 1995/True Science Music, 1995/Triple Gold Music, 1995/Jay King, IV, 1995/Chrysalis Songs, 1995/Warner-Tamerlane Music, 1995/Second Decade Music, 1995.
Best-selling record by Luniz from the album *Operation Stackola* (Noo Trybe, 95).

I Got I.D.
Words and music by Eddie Vedder.
Honest Music, 1995.
Best-selling record by Pearl Jam (Epic, 95).

I Hate Rock and Roll (English)
Words and music by William Reid.
Honey Music, 1995/BMC, 1995.
Introduced by The Jesus & Mary Chain on the album *The Jesus & Mary Chain Hate Rock and Roll* (American, 95).

I Hate You
Words and music by Prince (pseudonym for Prince Rogers Nelson).
Controversy Music, 1995/WB Music, 1995.
Best-selling record by Prince from the album *The Gold Experience* (NPG/Warner Brothers, 95).

I Have Something to Say to You
Words and music by Hugh Martin.
Revived by Michael Feinstein on the album *Michael Feinstein Sings the Hugh Martin Songbook* (Elektra Nonesuch, 95).

I Kissed a Girl
Words and music by Jill Sobule and Robin Eaton.
I'll Show You Music, 1995/Bug Music, 1995/Left Right Left Music, 1995/Warner-Tamerlane Music, 1995.
Best-selling record by Jill Sobule from the album *Jill Sobule* (Lava/Atlantic, 95).

I Know
Words and music by Milton Davis and William Duvall.
Sony Songs, 1994/Insofaras Music, 1994/Sony Music, 1994/GMMI Music, 1994.
Best-selling record by Dionne Farris from the film and soundtrack album *Ready to Wear* (Columbia, 94). Also featured on her album *Wild Seed--Wild Flower* (Columbia, 95).

I Let Her Lie
Words and music by Tim Johnson.
Little Dakota Music, Nashville, 1995/Big Giant Music, 1995/Privet Music, 1995.
Best-selling record by Daryle Singletary from the album *Daryle Singletary* (Giant/Warner Brothers, 95).

I Like
Words and music by John Howcutt, Emanual Officer, Donald Parks, and Tabitha Duncan.
Irving Music Inc., 1995/Nu Soul Music, 1995/Short Dolls Music, 1995.

Best-selling record by Kut Klose from the album *Surrender* (Keia/ Elektra, 95).

I Like It, I Love It
Words and music by Steve Dukes, Jeb Stuart Anderson, and Markus Hall.
Emdar Music, 1994/Texas Wedge, 1994/Rick Hall Music, 1994.
Best-selling record by Tim McGraw from the album *Not a Moment Too Soon* (Curb, 94).

I Live My Life for You
Words and music by Bill Leverty and C. J. Snare.
Sony Music, 1995/Wocka Wocka Music, 1995.
Best-selling record by Firehouse from the album *3* (Epic, 95).

I Miss You
Words and music by Vincent Herbert and Chuckie Howard.
Three Boys from Newark, 1994/Polygram International, 1994/Sure Light Music, 1994.
Best-selling record by N II U from the album *N II U* (Arista, 94).

I Refuse to Be Lonely
Words and music by Jud Friedman, Nick Martinelli, Alan Rich, and Phyllis Hyman.
MCA Music, 1994/All My Children Music, 1994/Command Performance Music, 1994/Music Corp. of America, 1994/Nelana Music, 1994/Music by Candlelight, 1994/PSO Ltd., 1994/ Schmoogietunes, 1994/Peermusic Ltd., 1994.
Best-selling record by Phyllis Hyman from the album *I Refuse to Be Lonely* (PIR, 95).

I Take You with Me
Words and music by Melissa Etheridge.
Black Keys, 1995/Hot Cha Music Co., 1995.
Introduced by Melissa Etheridge in the film and on the soundtrack album *Boys on the Side* (Arista, 95).

I Think about It All the Time
Words and music by Don Schlitz and Bill Livsey.
New Don Music, 1995/New Haven, 1995/Irving Music Inc., 1995.
Best-selling record by John Berry from the album *Standing on the Edge* (Capitol Nashville, 95).

I Walked
Words and music by Scott Sax.
Pepperstash Music, 1995.
Best-selling record by Wanderlust from the album *Wanderlust* (RCA, 95).

I Wanna Be Down
Words and music by Kevin Crouch and Kipper Jones.
Human Rhythm, 1994/Young Legend, 1994/Chrysalis Music Group, 1994.
Best-selling record by Brandy from the album *Brandy* (Atlantic, 94).

I Wanna Get Back with You
Words and music by Diane Warren.
Realsongs, 1994.
Introduced by Tom Jones and Tori Amos on the album *The Lead and How to Swing It* (Interscope/Atlantic, 94).

I Want You
Words and music by Anita Ross and Leon Ware.
Jobete Music Co., 1976/Black Keys, 1976.
Revived by Madonna and Massive Attack on the album *Inner City Blues: The Music of Marvin Gaye* (Motown, 95).

I Will
Words and music by John Lennon and Paul McCartney.
ATV Music Corp., 1968/Maclen Music Inc., 1968.
Revived by Ben Taylor in the film and on the soundtrack album *Bye Bye Love* (Giant/Warner Brothers, 95).

I Will Always Love You
Words and music by Dolly Parton.
Velvet Apple Music, 1974.
Revived by Dolly Parton and Vince Gill on the album *Souvenirs* (MCA, 95).

I Will Remember You (Canadian)
Words and music by Sarah McLachlan, Seamus Ennis, and Dave Merenda.
Sony Songs, 1995/Tyde, 1995/Seamus Ennis Music, 1995/Dave Mergenda Music, 1995.
Introduced by Sarah McLachlan in the film and on the soundtrack album *The Brothers McMullen* (Arista, 95).

I Wish
Words and music by Antoine Roundtree and Skee-Lo.
Orange Bear Music, 1995.
Best-selling record by Skee-Lo from the album *I Wish* (Sunshine/Scotti Brothers, 95).

Ice Cream (Incarcerated Scarfaces)
Words and music by Robert Diggs and C. Woods.
Careers-BMG, 1995/Ramecca Music, 1995/Wu-Tang Music, 1995.
Best-selling record by Chef Raekwon, guest starring Tony "Ghost Face

Killer" Starks from the album *Only Built 4 Cuban Linx* (Loud/RCA, 95).

I'd Be Lying
Words and music by Mary Karlzen.
Midwest Moon Music, 1995.
Introduced by Mary Karlzen on the album *Yelling at Mary* (Atlantic, 95).

I'd Lie for You (and That's the Truth)
Words and music by Diane Warren.
Realsongs, 1995.
Best-selling record by Meat Loaf from the album *Escape from Hell (Welcome to the Neighborhood)* (MCA, 95).

If I Never Knew You
Words and music by Alan Menken and Stephen Schwartz.
Walt Disney Music, 1995/Wonderland Music, 1995.
Introduced by Jon Secada and Shanice in the film and on the soundtrack album *Pocahontas* (Disney, 95).

If I Wanted To
Words and music by Melissa Etheridge.
MLE Music, 1994/Almo Music Corp., 1994.
Best-selling record by Melissa Etheridge from the album *Yes I Am* (Island, 94).

If I Were You
Words and music by John Hobbs and Chris Farren.
Soundbeam Music, 1994/Full Keel Music, 1994/Farrenuff, 1994.
Best-selling record by Collin Raye from the album *Extremes* (Epic, 94).

If the World Had a Front Porch
Words and music by Tracy Lawrence, Reid Neilsen, and Ken Beard.
TLE Music, 1994/Lac Grand Music, 1994/Muy Bueno Music, 1994/ Sony Tree Publishing, 1994/Terilee Music, 1994.
Best-selling record by Tracy Lawrence from the album *I See It Now* (Atlantic, 94).

If You Don't Love Me I'll Kill Myself
Words and music by Pete Droge.
Dead Man's Hat Music, 1994.
Introduced by Pete Droge on the album *Necktie Second* (American/ Reprise, 94). It's also featured in the film and on the soundtrack album *Dumb and Dumber* (RCA, 94).

If You Love Me
Words and music by Gordon Chambers, Nicole Gilbert, and Dave Hall.
Stone Jam Music, 1994/Ness, Nitty & Capone, 1994/Orisha Music,

1994/WB Music, 1994/Brown Girl Music, 1994/Night Rainbow
Music, 1994/EMI-April Music, 1994/Slow Flow Music, 1994.
Best-selling record by Brownstone from the album *From the Bottom Up*
(MJJ, 94).

If You Think You're Lonely Now
Words and music by Bobby Womack, Pat Moten, and Reg Griffin.
ABKCO Music Inc., 1981/Moriel, 1981.
Revived by K-ci Hailey in the film and on the soundtrack album
Jason's Lyric (Mercury, 94).

I'll Be Around
Words and music by Anthony Forte, Thom Bell, and B. Hurtt.
Rag Top, Oakland, 1994/Bellboy Music, 1994/Assorted Music, 1994/
Interscope Pearl, 1994/Warner-Tamerlane Music, 1994.
Best-selling record by Rappin' 4-Tay, featuring The Spinners, from the
album *Don't Fight the Feelin'* (Chrysalis, 94).

I'll Be over You
Words and music by Steve Lukather and Randy Goodrum.
BMG Music, 1994/California Phase Music, 1994.
Introduced by Larry Coryell (with Peabo Bryson and Grover
Washington) on the album *I'll Be over You* (CTI, 94).

I'll Be There for You
Words and music by David Crane, Marta Kaufman, Allee Willis, Phil
Solem, Danny Wilde, and Michael Skloff.
WB Music, 1994/Warner-Tamerlane Music, 1994.
Best-selling record by The Rembrandts from the TV show and
soundtrack album *Friends* (East/West, 95). It also appears on their
album *LP* (East/West, 95).

I'll Be There for You
Words and music by C. Smith and Robert Diggs.
Careers-BMG, 1995/Wu-Tang Music, 1995/Ramecca Music, 1995.
Best-selling record by Method Man and Mary J. Blige (Def Jam/RAL/
Island, 95).

I'll Make Love to You
Words and music by Babyface (pseudonym for Kenny Edmunds).
Sony Music, 1994.
Best-selling record by Boyz II Men from the album *II* (Motown, 94).

I'll Stick Around
Words and music by Dave Grohl.
MJ12 Music, 1995/EMI-Virgin, 1995.
Best-selling record by Foo Fighters from the album *Foo Fighters*
(Rosswell/Capitol, 95).

I'm Going Down
Words and music by Norman Whitfield and Joel Schumacher.
Duchess Music Corp., 1994.
Best-selling record by Mary J. Blige from the album *My Life* (Uptown/ MCA, 94).

I'm Gonna Be Strong
Words and music by Barry Mann and Cynthia Weil.
Screen Gems-EMI Music Inc., 1964.
Revived by Cyndi Lauper on the album *Twelve Deadly Cyns and Then Some* (Epic, 95).

I'm Not Strong Enough to Say No (English)
Words and music by Robert John "Mutt" Lange.
Zomba Music, 1995.
Best-selling record by BlackHawk from the album *Strong Enough* (Arista, 95).

I'm Still Dancin' with You
Words and music by Chick Rains and Wade Hayes.
Sony Tree Publishing, 1995.
Best-selling record by Wade Hayes from the album *Old Enough to Know Better* (DKC/Coliumbia, 95).

I'm the Only One
Words and music by Melissa Etheridge.
MLE Music, 1993/Almo Music Corp., 1993.
Best-selling record by Melissa Etheridge from the album *Yes I Am* (Island, 93).

Immortality
Words and music by Pearl Jam.
Honest Music, 1994/Write Treatage Music, 1994/Jumping Cat Music, 1994/Scribing C-Ment Music, 1994/Pickled Fish Music, 1994.
Best-selling record by Pearl Jam from the album *Vitalogy* (Epic, 95).

In Between Dances
Words and music by Craig Bickhardt and Barry Alfonso.
Almo Music Corp., 1995/Scarlet's Sister Music, 1995/Craig Bickhardt Music, 1995.
Best-selling record by Pam Tillis from the album *Sweetheart's Dance* (Arista, 95).

In Our Sleep
Words and music by Laurie Anderson.
Difficult Music, 1995.
Introduced by Laurie Anderson on the album *Bright Red* (Warner Brothers, 95).

In Pictures
Words and music by Joe Doyle and Bobby Boyd.
BMG Music, 1995/Careers-BMG, 1995.
Best-selling record by Alabama from the album *In Pictures* (RCA, 95).

In the Blood
Words˜ and music by Kevin Griffin.
Tentative Music, New Orleans, 1995.
Best-selling record by Better Than Ezra from the album *Deluxe* (Elektra, 95).

In the House of Stone and Light
Words and music by Martin Page.
EMI-Virgin, 1994.
Best-selling record by Martin Page from the album *In the House of Stone and Light* (Mercury, 94).

In This Life
Words and music by Mike Reid and Allen Shamblin.
Almo Music Corp., 1995/Brio Blues Music, 1995/Hayes Street Music, 1995/Allen Shamblin Music, 1995.
Introduced by Bette Midler on the album *Bette of Roses* (Atlantic, 95).

It's a Beautiful Life (Swedish)
English words and music by J. Berggren and John Ballard.
Mega Music, 1995/Careers-BMG, 1995.
Best-selling record by Ace of Base from the album *The Bridge* (Arista, 95).

It's Good to Be King
Words and music by Tom Petty.
Gone Gator Music, 1995.
Best-selling record by Tom Petty from the album *Wildflowers* (Warner Brothers, 95).

It's Too Late
Words and music by Carole King and Toni Stern.
Colgems-EMI Music, 1971.
Revived by Gloria Estefan on the album *Hold Me, Thrill Me, Kiss Me* (Epic, 94). Also revived by Amy Grant on the album *Tapestry Revisited: A Tribute to Carole King.*

J

J.A.R. (Jason Andrew Relva)
Words and music by Mike Dirnt, words and music by Green Day.
Green Daze, 1995/WB Music, 1995.
Introduced by Green Day in the film and on the soundtrack album
Angus (Reprise, 95).

Jealousy
Words and music by Liz Phair.
Sony Songs, 1995.
Introduced by Liz Phair on the album *Whip Smart* (Matador/Atlantic,
95).

Jeremy
Words and music by Eddie Vedder and Jeff Ament.
Innocent Bystander Music, 1992/Scribing C-Ment Music, 1992/Polygram
International, 1992.
Revived by Pearl Jam on the album *Ten* (Epic, 95).

Jersey Girl
Words and music by Tom Waits.
Fifth Floor Music Inc., 1980.
Revived by Holly Cole on the album *Temptation* (Metro Blue, 95).

Jesus Loves You, but Not as Much as I Do
Words and music by Eve's Plum.
Itchy Putschy, 1995/Warner-Tamerlane Music, 1995.
Introduced by Eve's Plum on the album *Cherry Alive* (550 Music/Epic,
95).

Jive Talking (English)
Words and music by Barry Gibb, Maurice Gibb, and Robin Gibb.
BMG Music, 1975.
Revived by The Blenders (Orchard Lane, 95).

K

Keep Their Heads Ringing
Words and music by Dr. Dre, Sam Sneed, and J. Flex.
Ain't Nothin' Goin on But Fu-kin, 1995.
Introduced by Dr. Dre in the film and on the soundtrack album *Friday* (Priority, 95).

Keeper of the Stars
Words and music by Dickie Lee, Danny Mayo, and Karen Staley.
Songs of Polygram, 1994/Paltime Music, 1994/New Haven, 1994/Pulpit Rock Music, 1994/Murrah, 1994.
Best-selling record by Tracy Byrd from the album *No Ordinary Man* (MCA, 94).

Kiss from a Rose
Words and music by Seal (pseudonym for Samuel Sealhenry).
SPZ, 1995.
Best-selling record by Seal from the film and soundtrack album *Original Music from the Motion Picture Batman Forever* (Atlantic, 95). It is also available on his album *Seal* (ZZT/Sire; Warner Bros., 94). Won Grammy Awards.

L

La La Means I Love You
Words and music by William Hart and Thom Bell.
Bellboy Music, 1968/Mighty Three Music, 1968.
Revived by Manhattan Transfer and Laura Nyro on the album *Tonin'*
(Atlantic, 95). Revived by Swing Out Sister on the album *The Living
Return* (Mercury, 95).

Lake Marie
Words and music by John Prine.
Weowna Music, 1995.
Introduced by John Prine on the album *Lost Dogs and Mixed Blessings*
(Oh Boy, 95).

Last Goodbye
Words and music by Jeff Buckley.
Sony Songs, 1995/El Viejito, 1995.
Introduced by Jeff Buckley on the album *Grace* (Columbia, 95).

Learn to Be Still
Words and music by Don Henley and Stan Lynch.
Songs of All Nations Music, 1995/WB Music, 1995/Night Rainbow
Music, 1995/Matanzas Music, 1995.
Best-selling record by The Eagles from the album *Hell Freezes Over*
(Geffen, 95).

Leave Virginia Alone
Words and music by Tom Petty.
Gone Gator Music, 1994.
Best-selling record by Rod Stewart from the album *A Spanner in the
Works* (Warner Brothers, 95).

Let Her Cry
Words and music by Mark Bryan, Dean Felber, Darius Rucker, and Jim
Sonnefeld.
Monica's Reluctance to Lob, 1994/EMI-April Music, 1994.

Best-selling record by Hootie & the Blowfish from the album *Cracked Rear View* (Atlantic, 94).

Let Me Be the One
Words and music by Eliot Sloan, Jeff Pence, and Emosia.
Hit & Run Music, 1995/Tosha Music, 1995/Barbosa Music, 1995/ Shapiro, Bernstein & Co., Inc., 1995.
Best-selling record by Blessid Union of Soul from the album *Home* (EMI, 95). Introduced on the TV show *All My Children*.

Let's Go to Vegas
Words and music by Karen Staley.
All Over Town, 1995/Sony Tree Publishing, 1995.
Best-selling record by Faith Hill from the album *It Matters to Me* (Warner Brothers, 95).

Life Gets Away
Words and music by Clint Black, Hayden Nicholas, and Tom Schuyler.
Blackened, 1995/Irving Music Inc., 1995/EMI-Blackwood Music Inc., 1995/Bethlehem Music, 1995.
Best-selling record by Clint Black from the album *Wishing for Christmas* (RCA, 95).

Life Goes On
Words and music by Idel Gray, Thom McHugh, and Keith Follese.
Howlin' Hits Music, 1995/Square West, 1995/Kicking Bird, 1995/ Thomahawk Music, 1995/Careers-BMG, 1995/Breaker Maker, 1995.
Best-selling record by Little Texas from the album *Greatest Hits* (Warner Brothers, 95).

Lightning Crashes
Words and music by Patrick Dahlheimer, Edward Kowalcyzk, Chad Gracey, and Chad Taylor.
Loco De Amor, New York, 1994/Audible Sun, New York, 1994.
Best-selling record by Live from the album *Throwing Copper* (Radioactive/MCA, 94).

Like a Rolling Stone
Words and music by Bob Dylan.
Special Rider Music, 1964.
Revived by The Rolling Stones on the album *Stripped* (Virgin, 95).

Like the Way I Do
Words and music by Melissa Etheridge.
Almo Music Corp., 1994/MLE Music, 1994.
Best-selling record by Melissa Etheridge from the album *Yes I Am* (Island, 94).

Like This and Like That
Words and music by Dallas Austin and Colin Wolfe.
EMI-April Music, 1995/D.A.R.P. Music, 1995/WB Music, 1995/
Nuthouse Music, 1995.
Best-selling record by Monica from the album *Miss Thang* (Rowdy/
Arista, 95).

A Little Bit of You
Words and music by J. Bruce and Craig Wiseman.
WB Music, 1995/Big Tractor, 1995/Almo Music Corp., 1995/Daddy
Rabbitt Music, 1995.
Best-selling record by Lee Roy Parnell from the album *Sometimes We
All Get Lucky* (Career, 95).

Little Miss Honky Tonk
Words and music by Ronnie Dunn and Don Cook.
Sony Tree Publishing, 1994/Showbilly, 1994.
Best-selling record by Brooks and Dunn from the album *Waitin' on
Sundown* (Arista, 94).

Little Things (English)
Words and music by Gavin Rossdale.
Mad Dog Winston Music, 1995/Truly Soothing Elevator Music, 1995.
Best-selling record by Bush from the album *Sixteen Stone* (Trauma/
Interscope, 95).

Live Forever (English)
Words and music by Noel Gallagher.
Sony Songs, 1994/Creation Music, 1994.
Best-selling record by Oasis from the album *Definitely Maybe* (Epic,
94).

Lonely Avenue
Words and music by Doc Pomus.
Unichappell Music Inc., 1956.
Revived by Los Lobos on the album *Until the Night Is Gone: A Tribute
to Doc Pomus* (Rhino, 95).

Long Road
Words and music by Eddie Vedder.
Innocent Bystander Music, 1992.
Best-selling record by Pearl Jam from the two-sided single *Merkinball*
(Epic, 95).

Long Snake Moan
Words and music by Polly Jean Harvey.
Hot Head Ltd. (England), 1995.
Introduced by P. J. Harvey on the album *To Bring You My Love* (Island,
95).

Long Voyage
Words and music by Hector Zazou.
Sony Music, 1995/John Cale, 1995.
Introduced by Suzanne Vega and John Cale on the album *Songs from the Cold Seas* (Columbia, 95).

Losing My Religion
Words and music by Bill Berry, Peter Buck, Mike Mills, and Michael Stipe.
Night Garden Music, 1991/Unichappell Music Inc., 1991.
Revived by Tori Amos in the film and on the soundtrack album *Higher Learning* (550 Music/Epic Soundtrax, 95). Also recorded by Rozalla on the album *Look No Further.*

Love Don't Need a Reason
Words and music by Peter Allen, Michael Callen, and Marsha Malamet.
Woolnough Music Inc., 1986/Warner-Tamerlane Music, 1986/Grand Alliance, 1986/Tops N Bottoms Music, 1986/Malamution Music, 1986.
Best-selling record by Marsha Malamet from the album *Love Worth Fighting For* (Theater Music, 95). Tune by the late Peter Allen was adopted as the unofficial anthem of various gay rights groups.

Love Me Still
Words and music by Bruce Hornsby and Chaka Kahn.
Basically Zappo Music, 1995.
Best-selling record by Chaka Kahn from the film and soundtrack album *Clockers* (MCA Soundtracks, 95). Nominated for a Grammy Award, Best Song for TV or Movie, 1995.

Love Spreads (English)
Words and music by John Squire.
Sony Music, 1994.
Best-selling record by Stone Roses from the album *Second Coming* (Geffen, 94).

Love TKO
Words and music by Cecil Womack and Gil Noble, Jr.
Warner-Tamerlane Music, 1980.
Revived by Regina Belle on the album *Reachin' Back* (Columbia, 95).

Love U for Life
Words and music by DeVante.
EMI-April Music, 1995/Deswing Mob, 1995.
Best-selling record by Jodeci from the album *The Show, the After Party, the Hotel* (Uptown/MCA, 95).

Love Will Keep Us Alive (American-English)
Words and music by Pete Vale, Jim Capaldi, and Paul Carrack.

Plangent Visions Music, Inc., London, England, 1994/EMI-Virgin, 1994/
    Freedom Songs Music, 1994/Warner-Tamerlane Music, 1994.
Best-selling record by The Eagles from the album *Hell Freezes Over*
    (Geffen, 94).

Lovin' Cup (Canadian)
Words and music by Jane Siberry.
MCA Music, 1995/Sold for a Song, 1995/Wing It, 1995.
Introduced by Jane Siberry on the album *Maria* (Reprise, 95).

Lump
Words and music by Chris Bellew, words and music by The Presidents
    of the United States.
Flying Rabbi Music, Seattle, 1995/David Dedderer, 1995.
Best-selling record by The Presidents of the United States from the
    album *The Presidents of the United States* (Popllama/Columbia, 95).

M

Mama Told Me Not to Come
Words and music by Randy Newman.
Unichappell Music Inc., 1966.
Revived by Wolfgang Press in the film and on the soundtrack album
Party Girl (Relativity, 95).

Man Who Sold the World
Words and music by David Bowie.
Tintoretto Music, 1972/Screen Gems-EMI Music Inc., 1972/South
Mountain Music Corp., 1972.
Revived by Nirvana on the album *MTV Unplugged in New York*
(Geffen, 94).

Maria
Words and music by Stephen Sondheim and Leonard Bernstein.
Chappell & Co., Inc., 1957/Leonard Bernstein Music, 1957.
Revived by Michael McDonald, James Ingram, and David Pack on the
album *The Songs of West Side Story* (RCA, 95).

Martha's Song
Words and music by Eric Mouquet and Michel Sanchez.
Sony Songs, 1995.
Introduced by Deep Forest on the album *Boheme* (550 Music/Epic, 95).

MC's Act Like They Don't Know
Words and music by Lawrence Parker and C. Martin.
Zomba Music, 1995/BDP Music, 1995/Gifted Pearl, 1995/EMI-April
Music, 1995.
Introduced by KRS-One on the album *KRS-One* (Jive, 95).

Mental Picture
Words and music by Jon Secada and Miguel Morejon.
Foreign Imported, 1994.
Best-selling record by Jon Secada from the album *Heart, Soul & a
Voice* (SBK, 94).

Mi Vida Loca (My Crazy Life)
Words and music by Pam Tillis and Jess Leary.
Ben's Future Music, 1994/Sony Tree Publishing, 1994/Dream Catcher
Music, 1994.
Best-selling record by Pam Tillis from the album *Sweetheart's Dance*
(Arista, 94).

Midnight at the Oasis
Words and music by David Nichtern.
Space Potato Music Ltd., 1973.
Revived by That Dog on the album *Spirit of '73: Rock for Choice* (Epic,
95).

Misery
Words and music by Dave Pirner.
LFR Music, 1995/WB Music, 1995.
Best-selling record by Soul Asylum from the album *Let Your Dim Light
Shine* (Columbia, 95).

Mishale
Words and music by Andru Donald and Eric Foster White.
WB Music, 1994/4MW Music, 1994/Zomba Music, 1994.
Best-selling record by Andru Donald from the album *Andru Donald*
(Metro/Blue/Capitol, 94).

Miss Sarajevo
Words and music by Bono (pseudonym for Paul Hewson) and Edge
(pseudonym for Dave Evans).
Polygram International, 1995.
Introduced by U2 and Placido Domingo in the film and on the
soundtrack album *Passengers* (Island, 95).

Missing
Words and music by Tracy Thorn and Ben Watt.
Sony Tree Publishing, 1995.
Best-selling record by Everything But the Girl from the album *The
Amplified Heart* (Atlantic, 95).

Molly (English)
Words and music by Sponge.
It Made a Sound Music, 1995/Plunkies, 1995/EMI-Virgin, 1995.
Best-selling record by Sponge from the album *Rotting Pinata* (Work/
Columbia, 95).

Moonlight
Words and music by John Williams, Alan Bergman, and Marilyn
Bergman.
F.S. Ltd., England, 1995/Grand Alliance, 1995/Marjer Publishing, 1995/
Threesome Music Co., 1995.

Introduced by Sting in the film and on the soundtrack album *Sabrina* (A & M, 95). Nominated for an Academy Award, Best Song of the Year, 1995.

More Human Than Human
Words and music by Rob Zombie (pseudonym for Rob Straker), words and music by White Zombie.
Psychohead Music, 1995/WB Music, 1995.
Best-selling record by White Zombie from the album *Astrocreep 2000* (Geffen, 95).

More Than a Feeling
Words and music by Tom Scholz.
Pure Songs, 1976.
Revived by Meow on the album *Goalie for the Other Team* (Enemy, 95).

Mother and Child Reunion
Words and music by Paul Simon.
Paul Simon Music, 1971.
Revived by Wailing Souls on the album *Live On* (Zoo/BMG, 95).

Murder Incorporated
Words and music by Bruce Springsteen.
Bruce Springsteen Publishing, 1982.
Revived by Bruce Springsteen on the album *Greatest Hits* (Columbia, 95).

Murder Was the Case
Words and music by Snoop Doggy Dogg (pseudonym for Calvin Broadus), Dr. Dre (pseudonym for Andre Young), Dat Nigga Daz (pseudonym for Delmic Arnaud), and Warren G.
WB Music, 1995/Sony Music, 1995.
Best-selling record by Snoop Doggy Dogg from the film and soundtrack album *Murder Was the Case* (Death Row/Interscope, 95).

My Body
Words and music by Cy Coleman and Ira Gasman.
Notable Music Co., Inc., 1995/Warner-Chappell Music, 1995.
Introduced by Leslie Gore on the album *The Life* (RCA, 95).

My Friends
Words and music by Anthony Kiedis, Flea (pseudonym for Michael Balzary), Dave Navarro, and Chad Smith.
Three Pounds of Love Music, 1995/EMI-Blackwood Music Inc., 1995.
Best-selling record by Red Hot Chili Peppers from the album *One Hot Minute* (Warner Brothers, 95).

My Generation
Words and music by Todd Snider.
Bro N' Sis Music, 1995/Keith Sykes Music, 1995.
Introduced by Todd Snider on the album *Songs for the Daily Planet*
(MCA, 95).

My Kind of Girl
Words and music by D. Cochran, John Jarrard, and Monte Powell.
Careers-BMG, 1994/Alabama Band Music Co., 1994/Wild Country
Music, 1994.
Best-selling record by Collin Raye from the album *Extremes* (Epic, 94).

My Love Is for Real
Words and music by Rhett Lawrence and Paula Abdul.
BMG Music, 1995/Rhett Rhyme Music, 1995/PJA Music, 1995.
Best-selling record by Paula Abdul from the album *Head over Heels*
(Captive/Virgin, 95).

My Name Is Jonah
Words and music by Rivers Cuomo.
E. O. Smith, West Los Angeles, 1994.
Introduced by Weezer on the album *Weezer* (Geffen, 94).

N

Naked Girl Falling down the Stairs
Words and music by Ivy Rorsach and Lux Interior.
Windswept Pacific, 1995/Longitude Music, 1995/Head Cheese, 1995.
Introduced by The Cramps on the album *Flamejob* (Medicine/Giant, 95).

Name
Words and music by Johnny Rzeznick.
EMI-Virgin, 1995/Full Volume Music, 1995/Scrap Metal Music, 1995.
Best-selling record by Goo Goo Dolls from the album *A Boy Named Goo* (Metal Blade/Warner Brothers, 95).

Natural One
Words and music by Lou Barlow, John Davis, and Walton Gagel.
Endless Soft Hits, Cambridge, 1995/Bliss WG Music, 1995.
Best-selling record by Folk Implosion from the film and soundtrack album *Kids* (London, 95).

Nature's Way
Words and music by Randy California.
Hollenbeck Music Co., 1970.
Revived by Victoria Williams on the album *Loose* (Mammoth/Atlantic, 95).

New Age Girl
Words and music by Caleb Guillote.
Nag, 1994/Songs of Polygram, 1994.
Best-selling record by Deadeye Dick from the film and soundtrack album *Dumb and Dumber* (RCA, 94).

New Girl in School
Words and music by Brian Wilson, Roger Christian, Jan Berry, and Bob Norman.
Screen Gems-EMI Music Inc., 1964.
Revived by Alex Chilton on the album *A Man Called Destruction* (Ardent, 95).

No Man's Land
Words and music by John Scott Sherrill and Steve Seskin.
Baby Mae Music, Austin, 1995/All Over Town, 1995/Sony Tree
    Publishing, 1995/New Wolf, 1995/Love This Town, 1995.
Best-selling record by John Michael Montgomery from the album *John Michael Montgomery* (Atlantic, 95).

No More I Love You's
Words and music by D. Freeman and J. Hughes.
Anxious Music, 1995/Careers-BMG, 1995.
Best-selling record by Annie Lennox from the album *Medusa* (Arista, 95).

Nobody Lives without Love
Words and music by Tonio K. (pseudonym for Steve Krikorian) and
    Larry Klein.
NYM, 1995/Jolene Cherry Music, 1995/WB Music, 1995/Little Reata,
    1995/Dee Klein Music, 1995.
Introduced by Eddi Reader in the film and on the soundtrack album
    Original Music from the Motion Picture Batman Forever (Blanco y
    Negro/Reprise, 95).

Not on Your Love
Words and music by Tony Martin, Reese Wilson, and Troy Martin.
Stroudacaster, 1995/Mark Alan Springer Music, 1995/Warner-Tamerlane
    Music, 1995.
Best-selling record by Jeff Carson from the album *Jeff Carson* (MCG/
    Curb, 95).

Nothing Sacred
Words and music by Jonatha Brooke and Alain Mallet.
Dog Dream, 1995/MCA Music, 1995.
Introduced by Jonatha Brooke & the Story on the album *Plumb* (Blue
    Thumb/GRP, 95).

Now They'll Sleep
Words and music by Tanya Donnelly and Christopher Gorman.
Slow Dog Music, 1995/Songs of Polygram, 1995/Mercer Street Music,
    1995.
Introduced by Belly on the album *King* (Sire/Reprise, 95).

Nowhere Man
Words and music by John Lennon and Paul McCartney.
Northern Songs, Ltd., England, 1966/Maclen Music Inc., 1966.
Revived by Randy Travis on the album *Come Together: America
    Salutes The Beatles* (Liberty, 95).

O

Ode to My Family (Irish)
Words and music by Noel Hogan and Delores O'Riordan.
Polygram International, 1994.
Best-selling record by The Cranberries from the album *No Need to Argue* (Island, 95).

Ol' 55
Words and music by Tom Waits.
Fifth Floor Music Inc., 1975.
Revived by Sarah McLachlan on the album *The Freedom Sessions* (Arista, 95).

Old Enough to Know Better
Words and music by Wade Hayes and Chick Rains.
Sony Tree Publishing, 1995.
Best-selling record by Wade Hayes from the album *Old Enough to Know Better* (Columbia, 95).

On a Bus to St. Cloud
Words and music by Gretchen Peters.
Sony Cross Keys Publishing Co. Inc., 1995/Purple Crayon Music, 1995.
Introduced by Trisha Yearwood on the album *Thinkin' about You* (MCA, 95).

On Grafton Street
Words and music by Nanci Griffith and Fred Koller.
Ponder Heart Music, 1994/Irving Music Inc., 1994/Polygram International, 1994/Door Number One, 1994/Plainclothes Music, 1994.
Introduced by Nanci Griffith on the album *Flyer* (Elektra, 95). Also recorded by Frances Black on the album *Talk to Me*.

One Boy, One Girl
Words and music by Mark Alan Springer and Shaye Smith.
EMI-Blackwood Music Inc., 1995/Maximum (Germany), 1995.

Best-selling record by Collin Raye from the album *I Think about You* (Epic, 95).

One Dream
Words and music by Emil Adler and Julie Flanders.
F.S. Ltd., England, 1995/October Project, 1995.
Introduced by October Project on the album *Falling Farther In* (Epic, 95).

One Emotion
Words and music by Clint Black and Hayden Nicholas.
Blackened, 1994/Irving Music Inc., 1994.
Best-selling record by Clint Black from the album *One Emotion* (RCA, 94).

One More Chance
Words and music by The Notorious B.I.G.
Big Poppa Music, 1995/Justin Publishing Co., 1995/EMI-April Music, 1995/Dan Penn Music, 1995.
Best-selling record by The Notorious B.I.G. from the album *Ready to Die* (Big Boy/Arista, 95).

One of Us
Words and music by Eric Bazilian.
Human Boy Music, 1995.
Best-selling record by Joan Osborne from the album *Relish* (Blue Gorilla/Mercury, 95). Nominated for Grammy Awards, Record of the Year, 1995 and Song of the Year, 1995.

One Sweet Day
Words and music by Mariah Carey, Michael McCary, Nathan Morris, Wayna Morris, Shawn Stockman, and Walter Afanasieff.
Sony Songs, 1995/Rye Songs, 1995/Black Panther, 1995/Vanderpool Music, 1995/Aynaw Music, 1995/Shawn Patrick Music, 1995/Grand Alliance, 1995.
Best-selling record by Mariah Carey and Boyz II Men from the album *Fantasy* (Columbia, 95). Nominated for a Grammy Award, Record of the Year, 1995.

The Only One I Love
Words and music by Christian Taylor.
30 Waldo Music, 1995/CLT Music, 1995/Mike & Alice Music, 1995/All Nations Music, 1995.
Introduced by Kurtin and Taylor on the TV show *General Hospital*.

Only Wanna Be with You
Words and music by Mark Bryan, Dean Felber, Darius Rucker, and Jim Sonnefeld.
Monica's Reluctance to Lob, 1994/EMI-April Music, 1994.

Best-selling record by Hootie & the Blowfish from the album *Cracked Rear View* (Atlantic, 94).

Orange Crate Art
Words and music by Van Dyke Parks.
You Call These Songs, 1994/Warner-Tamerlane Music, 1994.
Introduced by Brian Wilson and Van Dyke Parks on the album *Orange Crate Art* (Warner Brothers, 95).

P

Party Crowd
Words and music by Jimbeaux Hinson and David Lee Murphy.
American Romance Music, Nashville, 1995/N2D Publishing, 1995.
Best-selling record by David Lee Murphy from the album *Out with a Bang* (MCA, 95).

Peace and Love
Words and music by Neil Young.
Silver Fiddle, 1995.
Introduced by Neil Young on the album *Mirror Ball* (Reprise, 95).

Perry Mason
Words and music by Ozzy Osbourne, Zakk Wylde, and John Purdell.
Purdell Publishing, Glendale, 1995/Ozzy Osbourne Music, 1995/Zakk Wylde Music, 1995.
Introduced by Ozzy Osbourne on the album *Ozzmosis* (Epic, 95).

Pickup Man
Words and music by Howard Perdew and Kerry Kurt Phillips.
Songwriters Ink, 1994/Texas Wedge, 1994.
Best-selling record by Joe Diffie from the album *Third Rock from the Sun* (Epic, 94).

A Place Called Home
Words and music by Lynn Ahrens and Alan Menken.
Introduced by the cast in the musical *A Place Called Home*.

Playaz Club
Words and music by Anthony Forte.
Rag Top, Oakland, 1994.
Best-selling record by Rappin' 4-Tay from the album *Can't Fight the Feelin'* (Chrysalis, 94).

Player's Anthem
Words and music by The Notorious B.I.G., words and music by Little Kim and Little Caesar.

Undeas Music, 1995/EMI-April Music, 1995/Justin Publishing Co.,
  1995/Big Poppa Music, 1995/Clark's True Funk Music, 1995.
Best-selling record by Junior Mafia from the album *Conspiracy*
  (Underseas/Big Beat, 95).

Plowed (English)
Words and music by Sponge.
It Made a Sound Music, 1995/Plunkies, 1995.
Best-selling record by Sponge from the album *Rotting Pinata* (Work,
  95).

Possom Kingdom
Words and music by Todd Lewis.
Interscope Pearl, 1995/Warner-Tamerlane Music, 1995.
Best-selling record by Toadies from the album *Rubberman* (Interscope,
  95).

Power of Two
Words and music by Emily Saliers.
EMI-Virgin, 1994/Godhap Music, 1994.
Introduced by The Indigo Girls on the album *Swamp Ophelia* (Epic, 94).
  Also used in the film and on the soundtrack album *Boys on the Side*
  (Arista, 95).

Pretty Girl
Words and music by Babyface (pseudonym for Kenny Edmunds).
Sony Tree Publishing, 1995/Ecaf, 1995.
Best-selling record by Jon B. from the album *Bona Fide* (Yab Yum/550/
  Epic, 95).

Pure Massacre (English)
Words and music by Ben Gillies and Daniel Johns.
Best-selling record by Silverchair from the album *Frogstomp* (Epic, 95).

R

Rebecca Lynn
Words and music by Don Sampson and Skip Ewing.
MCA Music, 1995/Acuff Rose Music, 1995.
Best-selling record by Bryan White from the album *Bryan White*
(Asylum, 95).

Red Light Special
Words and music by Babyface (pseudonym for Kenny Edmunds).
Sony Music, 1994/Ecaf, 1994.
Best-selling record by TLC from the album *Crazysexycool* (LaFace/
Arista, 94). Nominated for a Grammy Award, Best R&B Song of the
Year, 1995.

Refried Dreams
Words and music by Jim Foster and Mark Peterson.
Zomba Music, 1994/Millhouse Music, 1994/Songs of Polygram, 1994.
Best-selling record by Tim McGraw from the album *Not a Moment Too
Soon* (Curb, 94).

Ridiculous Thoughts (Irish)
Words and music by Noel Hogan and Delores O'Riordan.
Polygram International, 1995.
Best-selling record by The Cranberries from the album *No Need to
Argue* (Island, 95).

River of Deceit
Words and music by Mad Season.
Jack Lord Music, Bainbridge Island, 1995/Wrecking Ball Music, Seattle,
1995/M. Marie Music, Los Angeles, 1995/Jumping Cat Music, 1995.
Best-selling record by Mad Season from the album *Above* (Columbia,
95).

Road Goes on Forever
Words and music by Robert Earl Keen.

Introduced by The Highwaymen on the album *The Road Goes on Forever* (Liberty, 95).

Rock and Roll Is Dead
Words and music by Lenny Kravitz.
Miss Bessie Music, 1995.
Introduced by Lenny Kravitz on the album *Circus* (Virgin, 95).

Rock and Roll Star (English)
Words and music by Noel Gallagher.
Creation Music, 1995/Sony Music, 1995.
Best-selling record by Oasis from the album *Definitely Maybe* (Epic, 95).

Roll Away
Words and music by Will Jennings and Martee Lebow.
MVH Too Music, 1995/Blue Sky Rider Songs, 1995/Irving Music Inc., 1995.
Introduced by Dusty Springfield on the album *A Very Fine Love* (Columbia, 95).

Roll to Me
English words and music by Justin Currie.
Polygram Music Publishing Inc., 1995.
Best-selling record by Del Amitri from the album *Twisted* (A & M, 95).

Romeo and Juliet (English)
Words and music by Mark Knopfler.
Almo Music Corp., 1980.
Revived by Cliff Eberhardt on the album *Mona Lisa Cafe* (Shanachie, 95).

Root Down
Words and music by The Beastie Boys.
Brooklyn Dust Music, 1995/Polygram International, 1995.
Best-selling record by The Beastie Boys from the album *Root Down* (Capitol, 95).

Run Around
Words and music by John Popper.
Blues Traveler Music, 1995/Irving Music Inc., 1995.
Best-selling record by Blues Traveler from the album *Four* (A & M, 95).

Run Away (German)
English words and music by Quickmix, Jai Wind, and Olaf Jeglitza.
Maximum (Germany), 1994.
Best-selling record by Real McCoy from the album *Real McCoy* (Arista, 94).

Runaway
Words and music by Janet Jackson, James Harris, III, and Terry Lewis.
Flyte Tyme Tunes, 1995/Black Ice Music, 1995.
Best-selling record by Janet Jackson from the album *Design of a Decade: 1986--1996* (A & M, 95).

S

Safe in the Arms of Love
Words and music by Mary Ann Kennedy, Pam Rose, and Pat Bunch.
Irving Music Inc., 1995/Fortunate Moon Music, 1995/LaRue Two
  Music, 1995/Zanesville Music, 1995.
Best-selling record by Martina McBride from the album *Wild Angels*
  (RCA, 95).

St. Teresa
Words and music by Rob Hyman, Eric Bazilian, Rick Chertoff, and
  Joan Osborne.
Human Boy Music, 1995.
Introduced by Joan Osborne on the album *Relish* (Blue Gorilla/Mercury,
  95).

San Francisco
Words and music by Van Dyke Parks.
You Call These Songs, 1995/Warner-Tamerlane Music, 1995.
Introduced by Brian Wilson and Van Dyke Parks on the album *Orange
  Crate Art* (Warner Brothers, 95).

Say It Ain't So
Words and music by Rivers Cuomo.
E. O. Smith, West Los Angeles, 1994.
Best-selling record by Weezer from the album *Weezer* (DGC, 95).

Scream
Words and music by Michael Jackson, Janet Jackson, James Harris, III,
  and Terry Lewis.
Mijac Music, 1995/Warner-Tamerlane Music, 1995/EMI-April Music,
  1995/Flyte Tyme Tunes, 1995/Black Ice Music, 1995.
Best-selling record by Michael Jackson from the album *HIStory* (Epic,
  95).

Secret Garden
Words and music by Bruce Springsteen.

Popular Music • 1995

Bruce Springsteen Publishing, 1995.
Introduced by Bruce Springsteen on the album *Greatest Hits* (Columbia, 95).

Send Me on My Way
Words and music by David Howard and Rusted Root.
Not of This World Music, 1995.
Best-selling record by Rusted Root from the album *When I Woke* (Mercury, 95).

Sense of Purpose (English)
Words and music by Chrissie Hynde.
Hynde House of Hits, England, 1995/Clive Banks, England, 1995/EMI Music Publishing, 1995.
Best-selling record by The Pretenders from the album *Isle of View* (Warner Brothers, 95).

Sensurround
Words and music by John Flansburgh and John Linnell.
TCF Music, 1995/They Might Be Giants Music, 1995.
Introduced by They Might Be Giants in the film and on the soundtrack album *The Mighty Morphin Power Rangers* (Atlantic, 95).

Sentimental
Words and music by Dallas Austin, Colin Wolfe, and Deborah Cox.
EMI-April Music, 1995/D.A.R.P. Music, 1995/WB Music, 1995/ Nuthouse Music, 1995/EMI-Blackwood Music Inc., 1995/Deborah Cox Music, 1995.
Best-selling record by Deborah Cox from the album *Deborah Cox* (Arista, 95).

Set U Free
Words and music by G. Acosta and Nadine Renee.
Nadine Renee Music, Miami Beach, 1995/Wax Head Publishing, Miami, 1995/New York House Music, 1995.
Best-selling record by Planet Soul (Strictly Rhythm Records, 95).

Sexual Healing
Words and music by Marvin Gaye, David Ritz, and Orville Brown.
EMI-April Music, 1973/Bug Pie Music, 1973/Ritz Rights Music, 1973/ EMI-Blackwood Music Inc., 1973.
Revived by Max-a-Million on the tribute album *Inner City Blues: The Music of Marvin Gaye* (SOS/Zoo, 95).

Shame
Words and music by John Finch and Reuben Cross.
Unichappell Music Inc., 1977/Mills & Mills, 1977.
Best-selling record by Zhane from the film and soundtrack album *A Low Down Dirty Shame*(Hollywood, 94).

She
Words and music by Billy Joe Armstrong, words and music by Green Day.
Green Daze, 1994/WB Music, 1994.
Best-selling record by Green Day from the album *Dookie* (Reprise, 94).

She Ain't Your Ordinary Girl
Words and music by Robert Jason.
Suzi Joe Music, Brentwood, 1994/My Split Music, Brentwood, 1994.
Best-selling record by Alabama from the album *Greatest Hits, Volume III* (RCA, 94).

She Don't Use Jelly
Words and music by Flaming Lips.
Lovely Sorts of Death Music, 1994/EMI-Blackwood Music Inc., 1994.
Best-selling record by Flaming Lips from the album *Transmissions from the Satellite Heart* (Warner Brothers, 94).

She's Every Woman
Words and music by Garth Brooks and Victoria Shaw.
BMG Songs Inc., 1995/Major Bob Music, 1995.
Best-selling record by Garth Brooks from the album *Fresh Horses* (Capitol, 95).

Shooting for the Moon
Words and music by Sonny Landreth.
Careers-BMG, 1995/Sonny Landreth Music, 1995.
Best-selling record by Sonny Landreth from the album *South of I-10* (Zoo, 95).

Should've Asked Her Faster
Words and music by Bob DiPiero, Al Anderson, and J. Klemick.
Al Andersongs, Nashville, 1995/Little Big Town, 1995/American Made Music, 1995/Mighty Nice Music, 1995.
Best-selling record by Ty England from the album *Ty England* (RCA, 95).

Shy Guy
Words and music by Diana King, Andy Marvel, and Kingsley Gardner.
Diana King Music, 1995/World of Andy's Music, 1995/Kingsley Gardner's Nation of Soul Music, 1995.
Best-selling record by Diana King from the film and soundtrack album *Bad Boys* (Work, 95).

Sick of Myself
Words and music by Matthew Sweet.
Charm Trap Music, 1995/EMI-Blackwood Music Inc., 1995.
Best-selling record by Matthew Sweet from the album *100% Fun* (Zoo, 95).

Simple Lessons
Words and music by Candlebox.
Maverick, 1995/Skinny White Butt, 1995/WB Music, 1995.
Best-selling record by Candlebox from the album *Lucy* (Maverick/ Warner Brothers, 95).

Sisters of Mercy
Words and music by Leonard Cohen.
Stranger Music Inc., 1967.
Revived by The Chieftains and Sting on the album *Tower of Song: A Tribute to Leonard Cohen* (A&M, 95).

Sleeping in the Flowers
Words and music by John Flansburgh and John Linnell.
They Might Be Giants Music, 1994/WB Music, 1994.
Introduced by They Might Be Giants on the album *John Henry* (Elektra, 94).

Slow Dancin'
Words and music by Jack Tempchin.
Warner-Chappell Music, 1975.
Revived by Gloria Loring on the album *Is There Anybody Out There* (Silk Purse, 94).

So Far Away
Words and music by Carole King and Toni Stern.
Colgems-EMI Music, 1971.
Revived by Rod Stewart on the album *Tapestry Revisited: A Tribute to Carole King* (Lava/Atlantic, 95).

So Help Me Girl
Words and music by Howard Perdew and A. Spooner.
Songwriters Ink, 1994/Texas Wedge, 1994.
Best-selling record by Joe Diffie from the album *Third Rock from the Sun* (Epic, 94).

Sold (The Grundy County Auction Incident)
Words and music by Richard Fagen and Robb Royer.
Of, 1995/Rob Roy West Music, 1995.
Best-selling record by John Michael Montgomery from the album *John Michael Montgomery* (Atlantic, 95).

Solitude
Words and music by Edwin McCain.
Harrington Music, 1995/EMI-April Music, 1995.
Best-selling record by Edwin McCain from the album *Honor among Thieves* (Lava/Atlantic, 95).

Some Cats Know
Words and music by Jerry Leiber and Mike Stoller.
Yellow Dog Music Inc., 1959.
Revived by Pattie Darcy Jones in the musical and on the cast album of
Smokey Joe's Cafe (Atlantic, 95).

Somebody's Cryin'
Words and music by Chris Isaak.
Chris Isaak Music Publishing, 1995.
Introduced by Chris Isaak on the album *Forever Blue* (Reprise, 95).

Someone Else's Star
Words and music by Skip Ewing and Jim Weatherly.
Acuff Rose Music, 1995/Mile Music, 1995.
Best-selling record by Bryan White from the album *Bryan White*
(Asylum, 95).

Someone to Love
Words and music by Babyface (pseudonym for Kenny Edmunds).
Sony Music, 1995/Ecaf, 1995.
Best-selling record by Jon B., featuring Babyface, from the film and
soundtrack album *Bad Boys* and the album *Bonafide* (Yab Yum/550/
Epic, 95). Nominated for a Grammy Award, Best Song for TV or
Movie, 1995.

Something 4 Da Honeyz
Words and music by Montell Jordan, Oji Pierce, and Doug Rasheed.
Mo Swang Music, 1995/Oji's Music, 1995/Mad Castle Music, 1995/
South Mountain Music Corp., 1995/Claude A. Music, 1995/Warner-
Tamerlane Music, 1995/Songs of Polygram, 1995/Second Decade
Music, 1995.
Best-selling record by Montell Jordan from the album *This Is How We
Do It* (PMP/RAL/Island, 95).

Something Inside So Strong
Words and music by L. Siffie.
MCA Music, 1995.
Introduced by The Rosa Parks Tribute Singers featuring Sounds of
Blackness, Vanessa Bell Armstrong, and Howard Hewitt (Vendy, 95).

Sometimes She Forgets
Words and music by Steve Earle.
WB Music, 1995.
Best-selling record by Travis Tritt from the album *Greatest Hits*
(Warner Brothers, 95).

Somewhere
Words and music by Stephen Sondheim and Leonard Bernstein.
Chappell & Co., Inc., 1957/Leonard Bernstein Music, 1957.

Revived by Phil Collins on the album *The Songs of West Side Story* (RCA, 95).

Somewhere in the Vicinity of the Heart
Words and music by Rick Chudacoff and Bill LaBounty.
Grand Alliance, 1994/Hidden Planet, 1994/Gouda Music, 1994/Buchu Music, 1994.
Best-selling record by Shenandoah and Alison Krauss from the album *Somewhere in the Vicinity of the Heart* (Capitol Nashville, 94).

Songbird
Words and music by Jesse Colin Young.
Pigfoot Music, 1975.
Revived by Dan Fogelberg and Tim Weisberg on the album *No Resemblance Whatsoever* (Giant/Warner Brothers, 95).

Soon as I Get Home
Words and music by Faith Evans, Chuckie Thompson, and Sean Combs.
Chyna Baby Music, 1995/Janice Combs, 1995/EMI-Blackwood Music Inc., 1995/Ninth Street Tunnel Music, 1995.
Best-selling record by Faith from the album *Faith* (Bad Boy/Arista, 95).

Soul City
Words and music by Rick Miller.
Monkey Dog, New York, 1995.
Introduced by Southern Culture on the Skids on the album *Dirt Track Date* (Geffen, 95).

Sour Times (English)
Words and music by Geoffrey Barrow, Betty Gibbons, Adrian Utley, Lalo Schifrin, Henry Brooks, and Otis Turner.
South Mountain Music Corp., 1994.
Best-selling record by Portishead from the album *Dummy* (Island, 94).

South of I-10
Words and music by Sonny Landreth.
Careers-BMG, 1995/Sonny Landreth Music, 1995.
Best-selling record by Sonny Landreth from the album *South of I-10* (Zoo, 95).

Standing on the Edge of Goodbye
Words and music by John Berry and Stewart Harris.
Kicking Bird, 1995/Sony Tree Publishing, 1995/Edisto Sound International, 1995.
Best-selling record by John Berry from the album *Standing on the Edge* (Patriot/Liberty, 95).

Stars
Words and music by Hum.

Martians Go Home Music, 1995.
Best-selling record by Hum from the album *You'd Prefer an Astronaut* (RCA, 95).

Starseed (Canadian)
Words and music by Chris Eacrett, Arnold Lanni, Maida Raini, and Mike Turner.
Lanni Tunes, 1995/Sony Tunes, 1995.
Best-selling record by Our Lady Peace from the album *Naveed* (Relativity, 95).

Strange Currencies
Words and music by Bill Berry, Peter Buck, Mike Mills, and Michael Stipe.
Night Garden Music, 1994/Warner-Tamerlane Music, 1994.
Introduced by R.E.M. on the album *Monster* (Warner Brothers, 94).

Strange World
Words and music by Ke (pseudonym for Kevin Grivois) and M. Pendergast.
Schizo Music, New York, 1995.
Introduced by Ke on the album *I Am* (RCA, 95).

Strong Enough
Words and music by Sheryl Crow, Bill Bottrell, David Baerwald, Kevin Gilbert, David Ricketts, and Brian Macleod.
Old Crow, Los Angeles, 1994/Warner-Tamerlane Music, 1994/Ignorant, 1994/Zen of Iniquity, 1994/Almo Music Corp., 1994/WB Music, 1994/Canvas Mattress, 1994/48/11 Music, 1994.
Best-selling record by Sheryl Crow from the album *Tuesday Night Music Club* (A&M, 94).

Stuck in the Middle with You
Words and music by Joe Egan and Gerry Rafferty.
Hudson Bay Music, 1973.
Revived by The Jeff Healey Band on the album *Cover to Cover* (Arista, 95).

Sugar Hill
Words and music by Az Barnes and K. Barnes.
Tricky Track Music, Piermont, 1995.
Best-selling record by AZ from the album *Doe or Die* (EMI, 95).

Summer's Comin'
Words and music by Clint Black and Hayden Nicholas.
Blackened, 1994/Irving Music Inc., 1994.
Best-selling record by Clint Black from the album *One Emotion* (RCA, 94).

Sun
English words and music by Roddy Frame.
WB Music, 1995.
Introduced by Aztec Camera on the album *Frestonia* (Reprise, 95).

Super Model
Words and music by David Baerwald, David Kitay, Brian McLeod, and
 Kristen Vigard.
F.S. Ltd., England, 1995/Zen of Iniquity, 1995/David Kitay Music,
 1995/Grand Alliance, 1995/Weenie Stand Music, 1995/Warner-
 Tamerlane Music, 1995/Five Piece Set Music, 1995.
Introduced by Jill Sobule in the film and on the soundtrack album
 Clueless (Lava/Atlantic, 95).

Sweet Old World
Words and music by Lucinda Williams.
Nomad-Noman, 1992/Ludakris, 1992/Warner-Tamerlane Music, 1992.
Revived by Emmylou Harris on the album *Wrecking Ball* (Reprise, 95).

Sympathy for the Devil (English)
Words and music by Mick Jagger and Keith Richards.
ABKCO Music Inc., 1968.
Revived by Guns N' Roses in the film and on the soundtrack album
 Interview with the Vampire (Geffen, 95).

T

Take a Bow
Words and music by Madonna (pseudonym for Madonna Ciccone) and
    Babyface (pseudonym for Kenny Edmunds).
Ecaf, 1994/Sony Music, 1994/Webo Girl, 1994.
Best-selling record by Madonna from the album *Bedtime Stories*
    (Maverick/Sire, 94).

Take Me to the River
Words and music by Al Green and Mabon Hodges.
JEC Publishing, 1973/Al Green Music, 1973.
Revived by Annie Lennox on the album *Medusa* (Arista, 95).

Tales from the Hood
Words and music by Domino and Victor Merrit.
South Mountain Music Corp., 1995/Ghetto Jam, 1995/All Init, 1995/
    Nike's Rap Music, 1995.
Introduced by Domino in the film and on the soundtrack album *Tales
    from the Hood* (MCA Soundtracks, 95).

Tell Me
Words and music by Bryce Wilson, Amel Larrieux, and Darryl Brown.
Almo Music Corp., 1995/Groove 78 Music, 1995/Jizop Music, 1995/
    Sony Tree Publishing, 1995/Dream Team Music, 1995.
Best-selling record by Groove Theory from the album *Groove Theory*
    (Epic, 95).

Tell Me I Was Dreaming
Words and music by Travis Tritt and Bruce Ray Brown.
Post Oak, 1994/Brass Crab Music, 1994.
Best-selling record by Travis Tritt from the album *Ten Feet Tall and
    Bulletproof* (Warner Brothers, 94).

Tell Me When (English)
Words and music by Paul Beckett and Phil Oakey.
MCA Music, 1995/EMI-Virgin, 1995.

Introduced by The Human League on the album *Octopus* (East West, 95).

Ten Storey Love Song (English)
Words and music by John Squire.
Sony Tunes, 1995.
Introduced by The Stone Roses on the album *Second Coming* (Geffen, 95).

Texas Tornado
Words and music by Bobby Braddock.
Sony Tree Publishing, 1994.
Best-selling record by Tracy Lawrence from the album *I See It Now* (Atlantic, 94).

Thank You
Words and music by Michael McCary, Nathan Morris, Wayna Morris, Shawn Stockman, and Dallas Austin.
Black Panther, 1994/Vanderpool Music, 1994/Aynaw Music, 1994/ Shawn Patrick Music, 1994/Grand Alliance, 1994/EMI-April Music, 1994/D.A.R.P. Music, 1994.
Best-selling record by Boyz II Men from the album *II* (Motown, 94).

That Ain't My Truck
Words and music by Tom Shapiro, Charlie Waters, and Rhett Akins.
Great Cumberland Music, 1995/Diamond Struck Music, 1995/Sony Tree Publishing, 1995.
Best-selling record by Rhett Akins from the album *A Thousand - Memories* (Decca, 95).

That Is Rock and Roll
Words and music by Jerry Leiber and Mike Stoller.
Yellow Dog Music Inc., 1959.
Revived by the cast of the musical *Smokey Joe's Cafe* (Atlantic, 95).

That's as Close as I'll Get to Loving You
Words and music by Seth Dworsky, Phil Jefferson, and Jan Layers.
McJames Music, 1995/I.R.S. Music, 1995/Bugle Publishing, 1995/Irving Music Inc., 1995/Almo Music Corp., 1995/Tikki Merm Music, 1995/ Siren Songs, 1995.
Best-selling record by Aaron Tippin from the album *Tool Box* (RCA, 95).

That's Just What You Are
Words and music by Aimee Mann and Jon Bryon.
Aimee Mann, 1995/You Can't Take It With You, 1995.
Best-selling record by Aimee Mann featured on the TV show and the soundtrack album *Melrose Place* (Giant, 95).

There Must Be a Better World Somewhere
Words and music by Doc Pomus and Mac Rebennack.
Stazybo Music, 1981/Skull Music, 1981.
Revived by Dr. John on the album *Afterglow* (Blue Thumb, 95).

They're Playin' Our Song
Words and music by John Jarrard, Mark D. Sanders, and Bob DiPiero.
Alabama Band Music Co., 1995/Wild Country Music, 1995/Miss Blyss
Music, 1995/Starstruck Writers Group, 1995/Mark D. Music, 1995/
Little Big Town, 1995/American Made Music, 1995.
Best-selling record by Neal McCoy from the album *You Gotta Love
That* (Atlantic, 95).

Thinkin' about You
Words and music by Bob Regan and Tom Shapiro.
Sierra Home, 1995/AMR, 1995/Great Cumberland Music, 1995/Lunn
Music Music, 1995.
Best-selling record by Trisha Yearwood from the album *Thinkin' about
You* (MCA, 95).

This Ain't a Love Song
Words and music by Jon Bon Jovi, Richie Sambora, and Desmond
Child.
Bon Jovi Publishing, 1995/Aggressive, 1995/Desmobile Music Inc.,
1995/Polygram International, 1995/EMI-April Music, 1995.
Best-selling record by Bon Jovi from the album *These Days* (Mercury,
95).

This House Is Not a Home
Words and music by Phil Solem, Danny Wilde, and Michael Skloff.
WB Music, 1995/Warner-Tamerlane Music, 1995.
Best-selling record by The Rembrandts from the album *LP* (EastWest,
95).

This Is a Call
Words and music by Dave Grohl.
MJ12 Music, 1995/EMI-Virgin, 1995.
Best-selling record by Foo Fighters from the album *Foo Fighters*
(Rosswell/Capitol, 95).

This Is How We Do It
Words and music by Montell Jordan, Oji Pierce, and R. Walters.
Mo Swang Music, 1995/Oji's Music, 1995/Def American Songs, 1995.
Best-selling record by Montell Jordan from the album *This Is How We
Do It* (PMP/RAL, 95).

This Lil' Game We Play
Words and music by Gerald Levert and Edwin Nicholas.
Divided, 1995/Zomba Music, 1995/Warner-Tamerlane Music, 1995/

Rampal, 1995.
Best-selling record by Subway, featuring 702, from the album *Good Times* (Biv 10/Motown, 95).

This Love Is Real
Words and music by John Prine.
Weowna Music, 1995.
Introduced by John Prine on the album *Lost Dogs and Mixed Blessings* (Oh Boy, 95).

This Time
Words and music by Mac McAnnally and Mark Miller.
Traveling Zoo, 1995/Beginner Music, 1995.
Best-selling record by Sawyer Brown from the album *Greatest Hits, 1990--1995* (Curb, 95).

This Woman and This Man
Words and music by Jeff Pennig and Michael Lunn.
Almo Music Corp., 1994/Bamatuck, 1994/WB Music, 1994/Lunn Music Music, 1994.
Best-selling record by Clay Walker from the album *If I Could Make a Living* (Giant, 94).

Til I Hear It from You
Words and music by Jessie Valenzuela, Rob Wilson, and Marshall Crenshaw.
Bonneville Salt Flats, 1995/Rude Corps Music, 1995/WB Music, 1995/ New Agency Music, 1995/Amalgamated Consolidated Music, 1995.
Best-selling record by The Gin Blossoms from the film and soundtrack album *Empire Records* (A & M, 95).

Til You Do Me Right
Words and music by Mel Edmunds, Kevon Edmunds, and Babyface (pseudonym for Kenny Edmunds).
Sony Music, 1995/Ecaf, 1995/Kmel Music, 1995.
Best-selling record by After 7 from the album *Reflections* (Virgin, 95).

Till You Love Me
Words and music by Bob DiPiero and Gary Burr.
Little Big Town, 1994/American Made Music, 1994/MCA Music, 1994/ Gary Burr Music, 1994.
Best-selling record by Reba McEntire from the album *Read My Mind* (MCA, 94).

Time
Words and music by Mark Bryan, Darius Rucker, Dean Felber, and Jim Sonnefeld.
Monica's Reluctance to Lob, 1994/EMI-April Music, 1994.

Best-selling record by Hootie & the Blowfish from the album *Cracked Rear View* (Atlantic, 94).

To My Own Devices
Words and music by Dave Pirner.
LFR Music, 1995/WB Music, 1995.
Introduced by Soul Asylum on the album *Let Your Dim Light Shine* (Columbia, 95).

Tom Courtenay
Words and music by Yo Lo Tengo.
Roshashauna, 1995/Excellent Classical Songs, 1995.
Introduced by Yo Lo Tengo on the album *Electr-o-Pura* (Matador, 95).

Tomorrow (English)
Words and music by Ben Gillies and Daniel Johns.
Best-selling record by Silverchair on the album *Frogstomp* (Epic, 95).

Tonight
Words and music by Stephen Sondheim and Leonard Bernstein.
Chappell & Co., Inc., 1957/Leonard Bernstein Music, 1957.
Revived by Kenny Loggins and Wynonna on the album *The Songs of West Side Story* (RCA, 95).

Tonite's the Night
Words and music by Jermaine Dupri, R. Parker, K. Harrison, T. Crum, R. Aikens, R. Neal, and C. Satchell.
So So Def Music, 1995/EMI-April Music, 1995/Globe Art Music, 1995/ Montezk Music, 1995/Play One Music, 1995/Rightsong Music, 1995.
Best-selling record by Kris Kross from the album *Young, Rich and Dangerous* (Ruffhouse/Columbia, 95).

Too Hot
Words and music by Artis Ivey, Jr., Brian Dobbs, and George Brown.
T-Boy Music Publishing Co., Inc., 1995/Boo Daddy, 1995/Wino Funk Music, 1995/Second Decade Music, 1995/Warner-Tamerlane Music, 1995.
Best-selling record by Coolio from the album *Gangsta's Paradise* (Tommy Boy, 95).

Total Eclipse of the Heart
Words and music by Jim Steinman.
EMI-Virgin, 1982.
Revived by Nicki French on the album *Secrets* (Critique, 95).

Tougher Than the Rest
Words and music by Bruce Springsteen.
Bruce Springsteen Publishing, 1987.
Revived by Chris LeDoux on the album *Haywire* (Liberty, 94).

Trial of the Century
Words and music by Cal Moregan.
Suds City Music, 1995.
Introduced by Cal & the Media Hounds (Calgar, 95).

Trouble
Words and music by Jacqueline Blake, Caroline Askew, and Conal
  Fitzpatrick.
Polygram International, 1995.
Introduced by Shampoo in the film and on the soundtrack album *The
  Mighty Morphin Power Rangers* (Atlantic, 95).

Turning Japanese (English)
Words and music by David Fenton.
Glenwood Music Corp., 1979.
Revived by Liz Phair on the album *Juvenalia* (Matator, 95).

Two Thousand Miles (English)
Words and music by Chrissie Hynde.
Hynde House of Hits, England, 1983/Clive Banks, England, 1983/EMI
  Music Publishing, 1983.
Revived by The Pretenders on the album *Isle of View* (Warner Brothers,
  95).

U

Universal Heartbeat
Words and music by Juliana Hatfield.
Zomba Music, 1995.
Best-selling record by Juliana Hatfield from the album *Only Everything*
(Mammoth/Atlantic, 95).

V

Victor/Victoria (American-English)
Words and music by Leslie Briccusse and Henry Mancini.
Stage & Screen Music Inc., 1981/EMI Variety Catalogue, 1981.
Revived by Julie Andrews and Tony Roberts in the musical
Victor/Victoria.

Violet
Words and music by Hole.
Mother May I, Sherman Oaks, 1994.
Introduced by Hole on the album *Live Through This* (DGC/Geffen, 94).

Vow
Words and music by Butch Vig, Duke Erickson, Shirley Manson, and
Steve Marker.
Vibe Crusher Music, 1995/Irving Music Inc., 1995/Dead Arm Music,
1995.
Best-selling record by Garbage from the album *Garbage* (Almo Sounds/
Geffen, 95).

W

The Waiting
Words and music by Tom Petty.
Gone Gator Music, 1981.
Revived by Linda Ronstadt on the album *Feels Like Home* (Elektra, 95).

Walk in the Sun
Words and music by Bruce Hornsby.
Basically Zappo Music, 1995.
Introduced by Bruce Hornsby on the album *Hot House* (RCA, 95).

Walk On
Words and music by Matraca Berg.
Patrick Joseph, 1990/Warner-Tamerlane Music, 1990/Samosonian
    Music, 1990.
Revived by Linda Ronstadt and Alison Krauss on the album *Feels Like
    Home* (Feels Like Home, 95).

Warm Love
Words and music by Van Morrison.
Caledonia Soul Music, 1973/WB Music, 1973.
Revived by General Public on the album *Rub It Better* (Epic, 95).

Warmth of the Sun
Words and music by Brian Wilson.
Rondor Music Inc., 1964.
Revived by Brian Wilson on the TV show and soundtrack album *I Just
    Wasn't Made for These Times* (Karambolage/MCA, 95).

Water Runs Dry
Words and music by Babyface (pseudonym for Kenny Edmunds).
Sony Music, 1994/Ecaf, 1994.
Best-selling record by Boyz II Men from the album *II* (Motown, 94).

Waterfalls
Words and music by Organized Noize, words and music by Marqueze
    Etheridge and Lisa Lopes.

Organized Noize Music, Atlanta, 1994/Stiff Shirt, 1994/Pettibone, 1994/ Tizbiz Music, 1994/Belt Star Music, 1994.
Best-selling record by TLC from the album *Crazysexycool* (LaFace/ Arista, 94). Nominated for a Grammy Award, Record of the Year, 1995.

Waydown (English)
Words and music by Catherine Wheel.
WB Music, 1995/Warner-Chappell Music, 1995.
Best-selling record by Catherine Wheel from the album *Catherine Wheel* (Fontana/Mercury, 95).

We Are Family
Words and music by Nile Rodgers and Bernard Edwards.
Bernard's Other Music, 1973/Skunk Deville, 1973/WB Music, 1973.
Revived by Babes in Toyland on the album *We Are Family* (Reprise, 95).

We're the Same
Words and music by Matthew Sweet.
Charm Trap Music, 1995/EMI-Blackwood Music Inc., 1995.
Introduced by Matthew Sweet on the album *100% Fun* (Zoo, 95).

What Mattered Most
Words and music by Gary Burr and Vince Melamed.
Gary Burr Music, 1995/August Wind Music, 1995/MCA Music, 1995/ Longitude Music, 1995/Albert Paw, 1995.
Best-selling record by Ty Herndon from the album *What Mattered Most* (Epic, 95).

What Was It You Wanted
Words and music by Bob Dylan.
Special Rider Music, 1992.
Revived by Chris Smither on the album *Up on the Lowdown* (Hightone, 95).

What Would You Say
Words and music by Dave Matthews.
Colden Grey Music, New York, 1994.
Best-selling record by The Dave Matthews Band from the album *Under the Table and Dreaming* (RCA, 94).

Whatever You Imagine
Words and music by Barry Mann, Cynthia Weil, and James Horner.
Dyad Music, Ltd., 1995/Fox Film Music Corp., 1995/TCF Music, 1995/ Raw Poo Music, 1995.
Introduced by Wendy Moten in the film and on the soundtrack album *The Pagemaster* (Fox Records, 94). Nominated for a Grammy Award, Best Song for TV or Movie, 1995.

When I Come Around
Words and music by Billy Joe Armstrong, words and music by Green
Day.
Green Daze, 1994/WB Music, 1994.
Best-selling record by Green Day from the album *Dookie* (Reprise, 94).

When You Say Nothing at All
Words and music by Don Schlitz and Paul Overstreet.
MCA Music, 1988/Don Schlitz Music, 1988/Screen Gems-EMI Music
Inc., 1988/Scarlet Moon Music, 1988.
Revived by Alison Krauss on the album *Keith Whitley: A Tribute Album*
(BNA, 94).

Where Ever You Are
Words and music by Denzil Foster and Thom McElroy.
Two Tuff-Enuff Music, 1995/EMI-Blackwood Music Inc., 1995.
Best-selling record by Terry Ellis from the album *Southern Gal* (East
West, 95).

Where I Used to Have a Heart
Words and music by Craig Bickhardt.
Hayes Street Music, 1993/Scarlet's Sister Music, 1993.
Best-selling record by Martina McBride from the album *The Way That I
Am* (RCA, 93).

Where's the Party At
Words and music by Doug E. Fresh.
Entertaining Music, New York, 1995.
Introduced by Doug E. Fresh on the album *Play* (Gee Street/
Independent, 95).

Wherever Would I Be
Words and music by Diane Warren.
Realsongs, 1995.
Introduced by Dusty Springfield and Daryl Hall in the film and on the
soundtrack album *While You Were Sleeping* (Columbia, 95).

Wherever You Go
Words and music by Clint Black and Hayden Nicholas.
Blackened, 1994/Irving Music Inc., 1994.
Best-selling record by Clint Black from the album *One Emotion* (RCA,
94).

Which Bridge to Cross (Which Bridge to Burn)
Words and music by Vince Gill and Bill Anderson.
Benefit Music, 1994/Stallion Music Inc., 1994/Sony Tree Publishing,
1994.
Best-selling record by Vince Gill from the album *When Love Finds You*
(MCA, 94).

Whiney Whiney (What Really Drives Me Crazy)
Words and music by Henry Mancini, David Raimer, Ray Davies, and Willie One Blood.
F.S. Ltd., England, 1995/Justin Combs Music, 1995/D.R., 1995/Jay-Boy Music Corp., 1995/Golden Rule Music, 1995.
Best-selling record by Willi One Blood from the film and soundtrack album *Dumb and Dumber* (RCA, 95).

Whiskey under the Bridge
Words and music by Don Cook, Kix Brooks, and Ronnie Dunn.
Sony Tree Publishing, 1994/Buffalo Prairie Songs, 1994/Don Cook, 1994/Showbilly, 1994.
Best-selling record by Brooks and Dunn from the album *Waitin' on Sundown* (Arista, 94).

A Whiter Shade of Pale
Words and music by Keith Reid and Gary Brooker.
TRO-Essex Music, Inc., 1967.
Revived by Annie Lennox on the album *Medusa* (Arista, 95).

Who Can I Run To
Words and music by Richard Roebuck, Charles Simmons, and Frank Alstin, Jr.
Warner-Tamerlane Music, 1995.
Best-selling record by Xscape from the album *Off the Hook* (So So Def/Columbia, 95).

Who Needs You Baby
Words and music by Clay Walker, Randy Boudreaux, and Kim Williams.
Lorrie Jayne, Nashville, 1995/Linda Cobb, Nashville, 1995/Sony Cross Keys Publishing Co. Inc., 1995/That's a Smash Music, 1995.
Best-selling record by Clay Walker from the album *Hypnotize the Moon* (Giant/Warner Brothers, 95).

Whose Bed Have Your Boots Been Under (English)
Words and music by Robert John "Mutt" Lange and Shania Twain.
Loon Echo Music, 1995/Zomba Music, 1995.
Best-selling record by Shania Twain from the album *The Woman in Me* (Mercury Nashville, 95).

Why Walk When You Can Fly
Words and music by Mary Chapin Carpenter.
Why Walk, 1993.
Best-selling record by Mary Chapin Carpenter from the album *Stones in the Road* (Columbia, 93).

Wild Night (English)
Words and music by Van Morrison.

WB Music, 1971/Caledonia Soul Music, 1971.
Revived by John Mellencamp and Me'Shell NdegeOcello on the album *Dance Naked* (Mercury, 94).

The Woman in Me Needs the Man in You (English)
Words and music by Robert John "Mutt" Lange and Shania Twain.
Loon Echo Music, 1995/Zomba Music, 1995.
Best-selling record by Shania Twain from the album *The Woman in Me* (Mercury Nashville, 95).

Woman to Woman
Words and music by James Banks, Eddie Marion, and Henderson Thigpen.
Irving Music Inc., 1974.
Revived by Jewell in the film and on the soundtrack album *Murder Was the Case* (Death Row/Interscope, 95).

Wonder
Words and music by Natalie Merchant.
Indian Love Bride Music, New York, 1995.
Best-selling record by Natalie Merchant from the album *Carnival* (Elektra, 95).

Wonderful (English)
Words and music by Adam Ant (pseudonym for Stuart Goddard), Marco Pironi, and Bonnie Hayes.
EMI Music Publishing, 1995/Colgems-EMI Music, 1995/Firstars Music, 1995/Almo Music Corp., 1995.
Best-selling record by Adam Ant from the album *Wonderful* (Capitol, 95).

Wonderwall (English)
Words and music by Noel Gallagher.
Sony Songs, 1995/Creation Music, 1995.
Best-selling record by Oasis from the album *What's the Story Morning Glory* (Epic, 95).

The World I Know
Words and music by Ed Roland.
Roland/Lentz, New York, 1995/Warner-Chappell Music, 1995.
Best-selling record by Collective Soul from the album *Collective Soul* (Atlantic, 95).

Wrecking Ball
Words and music by Neil Young.
Silver Fiddle, 1995.
Introduced by Neil Young on the album *Mirror Ball* (Reprise, 95).
Revived by Emmylou Harris on the album *Wrecking Ball* (Reprise, 95).

Y

Yellow Ledbetter
Words and music by Eddie Vedder and Jeff Ament.
Innocent Bystander Music, 1994/Scribing C-Ment Music, 1994/Polygram
 International, 1994.
Best-selling record by Pearl Jam (Epic, 95).

You Ain't Much Fun
Words and music by Toby Keith and C. Goff, Jr.
Songs of Polygram, 1994/Tokeco, 1994.
Best-selling record by Toby Keith from the album *Boomtown* (Polydor,
 94).

You Are Not Alone
Words and music by Robert Kelly and Michael Jackson.
Zomba Music, 1995/Mijac Music, 1995.
Best-selling record by Michael Jackson from the album *HIStory* (MJJ/
 Epic, 95). Nominated for a Grammy Award, Song of the Year, 1995.

You Better Think Twice
Words and music by Vince Gill and Reid Neilsen.
Benefit Music, 1994/Longitude Music, 1994.
Best-selling record by Vince Gill from the album *When Love Finds You*
 (MCA, 94).

You Can Sleep While I Drive
Words and music by Melissa Etheridge.
Almo Music Corp., 1989/MLE Music, 1989.
Revived by Trisha Yearwood on the album *Thinkin' about You* (MCA,
 95).

You Can't Make a Heart Love Somebody
Words and music by Steve Clark and Johnny MacRae.
Victoria Kay Music, 1994/BMG Music, 1994/Little Beagle Music, 1994.
Best-selling record by George Strait from the album *Lead On* (MCA,
 94).

You Can't Run
Words and music by Babyface (pseudonym for Kenny Edmunds).
Ecaf, 1994/Sony Music, 1994.
Best-selling record Vanessa Williams from the album *The Sweetest Days* (Wing/Mercury, 94). Nominated for a Grammy Award, Best R&B Song of the Year, 1995.

You Don't Even Know Who I Am
Words and music by Gretchen Peters.
Sony Cross Keys Publishing Co. Inc., 1994/Purple Crayon Music, 1994.
Best-selling record by Patty Loveless from the album *When Fallen Angels Fly* (Epic, 94). Nominated for a Grammy Award, Best Country Song of the Year, 1995.

You Don't Know How It Feels
Words and music by Tom Petty.
Gone Gator Music, 1994.
Best-selling record by Tom Petty from the album *Wildflowers* (Warner Brothers, 94).

You Got It
Words and music by Tom Petty, Jeff Lynne, and Roy Orbison.
Gone Gator Music, 1989/EMI-April Music, 1989/Orbisongs, 1989.
Revived by Bonnie Raitt in the film and on the soundtrack album *Boys on the Side* (Arista, 95).

You Gotta Be (English)
Words and music by Des'ree and Ashley Ingram.
Sony Music, 1994.
Best-selling record by Des'ree from the album *I Ain't Movin'* (550 Music, 94).

You Have the Right to Remain Silent
Words and music by Brenda Sweat and Calvin Sweat.
Co-Heart Music, 1995.
Best-selling record by Perfect Stranger from the album *You Have the Right to Remain Silent* (Curb, 95).

You Oughta Know
Words and music by Glen Ballard and Alanis Morissette.
MCA Music, 1995/Van Hurst Place Music, 1995/Aerostation Corp., 1995.
Best-selling record by Alanis Morissette from the album *Jagged Little Pill* (Maverick/Reprise, 95). Won a Grammy Award for Best Rock Song of the Year 1995. Nominated for a Grammy Award, Song of the Year, 1995.

You R' Loved
Words and music by Victoria Williams.

Mumblety Peg, 1995/Careers-BMG, 1995.
Introduced by Victoria Williams on the album *Loose* (Mammoth/ Atlantic, 95).

You Remind Me of Something
Words and music by Robert Kelly.
Zomba Music, 1995/R. Kelly Music, 1995.
Best-selling record by R. Kelly from the album *R. Kelly* (Jive, 95).

You Used to Love Me
Words and music by Faith Evans.
EMI-April Music, 1995/Ninth Street Tunnel Music, 1995/Chyna Baby
   Music, 1995/Janice Combs, 1995/EMI-Blackwood Music Inc., 1995/
   Maximum (Germany), 1995.
Best-selling record by Faith from the album *Faith* (Bad Boy/Arista, 95).

You Wreck Me
Words and music by Tom Petty.
Gone Gator Music, 1994.
Best-selling record by Tom Petty from the album *Wildflowers* (Warner
   Brothers, 94).

You'll See
Words and music by David Foster and Madonna (pseudonym for
   Madonna Ciccone).
WB Music, 1995/Webo Girl, 1995/One Four Three, 1995/Break of
   Dawn Music Inc., 1995/Peer Five Music, 1995.
Best-selling record by Madonna from the album *Something to
   Remember* (Maverick/Warner Brothers, 95).

Youngstown
Words and music by Bruce Springsteen.
Bruce Springsteen Publishing, 1995.
Introduced by Bruce Springsteen on the album *The Ghost of Tom Joad*
   (Columbia, 95).

Your Little Secret
Words and music by Melissa Etheridge.
Almo Music Corp., 1995/MLE Music, 1995.
Best-selling record by Melissa Etheridge from the album *Your Little
   Secret* (Island, 95).

You're Gonna Miss Me When I'm Gone
Words and music by Kix Brooks, Don Cook, and Ronnie Dunn.
Sony Tree Publishing, 1994/Buffalo Prairie Songs, 1994/Showbilly,
   1994/Don Cook, 1994.
Best-selling record by Brooks and Dunn from the album *Waitin' on
   Sundown* (Arista, 94).

Popular Music ● 1995

You've Got a Friend
Words and music by Carole King.
Screen Gems-EMI Music Inc., 1971.
Revived by Bebe and Cece Winans and Aretha Franklin on the album
Tapestry Revisited: A Tribute to Carole King (Lava/Atlantic, 95).

You've Got a Friend in Me
Words and music by Randy Newman.
Walt Disney Music, 1995.
Introduced by Randy Newman and Lyle Lovett in the film and on the
soundtrack album *Toy Story* (Disney, 95). Nominated for an Academy
Award, Best Song, 1995.

Z

Zombie (Irish)
Words and music by Noel Hogan and Delores O'Riordan.
Polygram International, 1994.
Best-selling record by The Cranberries from the album *No Need to Argue* (Island, 94).

Lyricists & Composers Index

Lyricists & Composers Index

Lyricists & Composers Index

Lyricists & Composers Index

Lyricists & Composers Index

Lyricists & Composers Index

Lyricists & Composers Index

Important Performances Index

Songs are listed under the works in which they were introduced or given significant renditions. The index is organized into major sections by performance medium: Album, Movie, Musical, Performer, Revue, Television Show.

Album

Above
  River of Deceit
Adios Amigos!
  I Don't Want to Grow Up
Afterglow
  There Must Be a Better World Somewhere
Ain't Had Enough Fun
  Borderline Blues
Ain't Nothin' but a She Thing
  Ain't Nothin' but a She Thing
All I Want
  Can't Really Be Gone
American Standard
  Cumbersome
The Amplified Heart
  Missing
Andru Donald
  Mishale
Angus
  J.A.R. (Jason Andrew Relva)
Another Night
  Come and Get Your Love
Anthology I
  Free as a Bird

Astrocreep 2000
  More Human Than Human
Aurora Gory Alice
  Here and Now
Azz Izz
  He's Mine
Back for Good
  Back for Good
Bad Boys
  Shy Guy
  Someone to Love
Balance
  Can't Stop Loving You
  Don't Tell Me (What Love Can Do)
Ball-Hog or Tugboat
  Against the 70s
Ballbreaker
  Hard as a Rock
Bedtime Stories
  Take a Bow
Bette of Roses
  In This Life
Big Ones
  Blind Man
Boheme
  Martha's Song

121

Important Performances Index — Album

Under the Table and Dreaming
  Ants Marching
  What Would You Say
Until the Night Is Gone: A Tribute to
  Doc Pomus
  Lonely Avenue
Up on the Lowdown
  What Was It You Wanted
A Very Fine Love
  Roll Away
Vitalogy
  Better Man
  Corduroy
  Immortality
Waitin' on Sundown
  Little Miss Honky Tonk
  Whiskey under the Bridge
  You're Gonna Miss Me When I'm
    Gone
Waiting to Exhale
  Exhale (Shoop Shoop)
Wanderlust
  I Walked
The Way That I Am
  Where I Used to Have a Heart
We Are Family
  We Are Family
Weezer
  My Name Is Jonah
  Say It Ain't So
Whaler
  As I Lay Me Down
What a Crying Shame
  All That Heaven Will Allow
What a Way to Live
  Goin' through the Big D
  Gonna Get a Life
What Mattered Most
  What Mattered Most
What's the Story Morning Glory
  Wonderwall
When Fallen Angels Fly
  Here I Am
  You Don't Even Know Who I Am
When I Woke
  Send Me on My Way
When Love Finds You
  Go Rest High on That Mountain

Which Bridge to Cross (Which Bridge
  to Burn)
  You Better Think Twice
While You Were Sleeping
  Wherever Would I Be
Whip Smart
  Jealousy
Who I Am
  Gone Country
  I Don't Even Know Your Name
Wholesale Meat and Fish
  Awake
Wigstock
  Free to Be
Wild Angels
  Safe in the Arms of Love
Wild Seed--Wild Flower
  Don't Ever Touch Me (Again)
  I Know
Wildflowers
  It's Good to Be King
  You Don't Know How It Feels
  You Wreck Me
Wishing for Christmas
  Life Gets Away
The Woman in Me
  Any Man of Mine
  Whose Bed Have Your Boots Been
    Under
  The Woman in Me Needs the Man in
    You
Wonderful
  Wonderful
Wrecking Ball
  Every Grain of Sand
  Sweet Old World
  Wrecking Ball
Yelling at Mary
  I'd Be Lying
Yes
  Honey White
Yes I Am
  If I Wanted To
  I'm the Only One
  Like the Way I Do
You Gotta Love That
  For a Change
  They're Playin' Our Song

Important Performances Index — Movie

The Show
  How High
Tales from the Hood
  Tales from the Hood
To Wong Foo, Love Julie Newmar
  Hey Now (Girls Just Want to Have
    Fun)
Toy Story
  You've Got a Friend in Me
Waiting to Exhale
  Exhale (Shoop Shoop)
While You Were Sleeping
  Wherever Would I Be
Wigstock
  Free to Be

Musical
A Place Called Home
  A Place Called Home
Smokey Joe's Cafe
  Some Cats Know
  That Is Rock and Roll
Victor/Victoria
  Crazy World
  Victor/Victoria

Performer
Abdul, Paula
  Crazy Cool
  My Love Is for Real
AC/DC
  Hard as a Rock

Ace of Base

  It's a Beautiful Life
Adams, Bryan
  Have You Ever Really Loved a
    Woman
Aerosmith
  Blind Man
After 7
  Til You Do Me Right
Akins, Rhett
  That Ain't My Truck
Alabama
  Give Me One More Shot

In Pictures
  She Ain't Your Ordinary Girl
Alison Krauss & Union Station
  Baby Now That I've Found You
Amos, Tori
  I Wanna Get Back with You
  Losing My Religion
Anderson, John
  Bend It until It Breaks
Anderson, Laurie
  In Our Sleep
Andrews, Julie
  Crazy World
  Victor/Victoria
Ant, Adam
  Wonderful
Armstrong, Vanessa Bell
  Something Inside So Strong
Austin, Patti
  Cool
AZ
  Sugar Hill
Aztec Camera
  Sun
B., Stevie
  Dream about You
Babes in Toyland
  We Are Family
Babyface
  Someone to Love
The Beastie Boys
  Root Down
The Beatles
  Baby It's You
  Free as a Bird
Belle, Regina
  Love TKO
Belly
  Now They'll Sleep
Bernard, Crystal
  (It Won't Take) Forever Tonight
Berry, John
  I Think about It All the Time
  Standing on the Edge of Goodbye
Better Than Ezra
  Good
  In the Blood

132

Television Show

Awards Index

A list of songs nominated for Academy Awards by the Academy of Motion Picture Arts and Sciences and Grammy Awards from the National Academy of Recording Arts and Sciences. Asterisks indicate the winners; multiple listings indicate multiple nominations.

1995

Academy Award
  Colors of the Wind*
  Dead Man Walking
  Have You Ever Really Loved a
    Woman
  Moonlight
  You've Got a Friend in Me
Grammy Award
  Any Man of Mine
  Brown Sugar
  Colors of the Wind*
  Creep
  Dignity
  Downtown
  For Your Love*
  Gangsta's Paradise
  Go Rest High on That Mountain*
Gone Country
Have You Ever Really Loved a
  Woman
Hold Me, Thrill Me, Kiss Me, Kill Me
Hurt
I Can Love You Like That
Kiss from a Rose*
Love Me Still
One of Us
One Sweet Day
Red Light Special
Someone to Love
Waterfalls
Whatever You Imagine
You Are Not Alone
You Can't Run
You Don't Even Know Who I Am
You Oughta Know
You Oughta Know*

List of Publishers

A directory of publishers of the songs included in *Popular Music,* 1995. Publishers that are members of the American Society of Composers, Authors, and Publishers or whose catalogs are available under ASCAP license are indicated by the designation (ASCAP). Publishers that have granted performing rights to Broadcast Music, Inc., are designated by the notation (BMI). Publishers whose catalogs are represented by The Society of Composers, Authors and Music Publishers of Canada, are indicated by the designation (SOCAN).

The addresses were gleaned from a variety of sources, including ASCAP, BMI, SOCAN, and *Billboard* magazine. As in any volatile industry, many of the addresses may become outdated quickly. In the interim between the book's completion and its subsequent publication, some publishers may have been consolidated into others or changed hands. This is a fact of life long endured by the music business and its constituents. The data collected here, and throughout the book, are as accurate as such circumstances allow.

A

ABKCO Music Inc. (BMI)
1700 Broadway
New York, New York 10019

Acuff Rose Music (BMI)
65 Music Square West
Nashville, Tennessee 37203

Aerostation Corp. (ASCAP)
16214 Morrison St.
Encino, California 91436

Afro Dredite Music (BMI)
see Better Than Your Music

Aggressive (ASCAP)
see EMI Music Publishing

Ah Choo (ASCAP)
see PolyGram Records Inc.

Ain't Nothin' Goin on But Fu-kin (ASCAP)
see Sony Music

Air Control (ASCAP)
see EMI Music Publishing

Al Andersongs (BMI)
PO Box 120904
Nashville, Tennessee 37212

Alabama Band Music Co. (ASCAP)
PO Box 121192
Nashville, Tennessee 37212

List of Publishers

Albert Paw (BMI)
see Longitude Music

All Init (ASCAP)
see Chrysalis Music Group

All My Children Music (ASCAP)
see MCA Music

All Nations Music (ASCAP)
8857 W. Olympic Blvd., Ste. 200
Beverly Hills, California 90211

All Over Town (BMI)
see Sony Tree Publishing

Almo/Irving
1358 N. LaBrea
Los Angeles, California 90028

Almo/Irving Music (BMI)
1358 N La Brea
Los Angeles, California 90028

Almo Music Corp. (BMI)
360 N. La Cienega
Los Angeles, California 90048

Amalgamated Consolidated Music (ASCAP)
see Warner-Chappell Music

American Made Music (BMI)
c/o Little Big Town Music
803 18th Ave., S.
Nashville, Tennessee 37203

American Romance Music (ASCAP)
c/o CMI America
1102 17th Ave. S., Ste. 401
Nashville, Tennessee 37212

AMR (ASCAP)
54 Music Sq. E.
Nashville, Tennessee 37203

Anxious Music (BMI)
see BMG Music

Any Kind of Music (BMI)
see MCA Music

Arvemal Music (ASCAP)
see EMI Music Publishing

Assorted Music (BMI)
Attn: Earl Shelton
309 S. Broad St.
Philadelphia, Pennsylvania 19107

ATV Music Corp. (BMI)
see MCA, Inc.

Audible Sun (BMI)
1775 Broadway, 7th Fl.
New York, New York 10019

August Wind Music (BMI)
see Longitude Music

Avant Garde Music (ASCAP)
Box 92004
Los Angeles, California 90009

Aynaw Music (BMI)
see Famous Music Corp.

B

B and It Is Music (BMI)
see Turkishman

Baby Mae Music (BMI)
c/o Hamstein
PO Box 163870
Austin, Texas 78716

Badams Music (ASCAP)
see Almo Music Corp.

Bamatuck (ASCAP)
21 Music Square East
Nashville, Tennessee 37203

Barbosa Music (ASCAP)
see Hit & Run Music

Basically Zappo Music (ASCAP)
see Warner-Chappell Music

BDP Music (ASCAP)
see Zomba Music

Bee Mo Easy (ASCAP)
see EMI Music Publishing

Beginner Music (ASCAP)
PO Box 50418
Nashville, Tennessee 37205

Bellarmine Music (BMI)
see Maypop Music

Bellboy Music (BMI)
Attn: Earl Shelton
309 S. Broad St.
Philadelphia, Pennsylvania 19107

Maria Belle (BMI)
see Warner-Chappell Music

Belt Star Music (ASCAP)
see Turkishman

Benefit Music (BMI)
7250 Beverly Blvd
Los Angeles, California 90036

Ben's Future Music (BMI)
see Sony Music

Bernard's Other Music (BMI)
see Warner-Chappell Music

Leonard Bernstein Music (ASCAP)
see Warner-Chappell Music

Bertam Music Co. (ASCAP)
see Jobete Music Co.

Bethlehem Music (BMI)
see EMI Music Publishing

Better Than Your Music (BMI)
see Warner-Chappell Music

Craig Bickhardt Music
see Almo/Irving

Big Giant Music (BMI)
see Warner-Chappell Music

Big Herb Music (BMI)
see EMI Music Publishing

Big Poppa Music (ASCAP)
see EMI Music Publishing

Big Tractor (ASCAP)
see Warner-Chappell Music

Black Cypress Music (ASCAP)
see Warner-Chappell Music

Black Ice Music (BMI)
see Flyte Tyme Tunes

Black Keys (BMI)
PO Box 3633
Thousand Oaks, California 91360

Black Panther (BMI)
see Famous Music Corp.

Blackened (BMI)
c/o Prager & Fenton
12424 Wilshire Blvd., Ste. 1000
Los Angeles, California 90025

Bliss WG Music (ASCAP)
Address Unavailable

Blue Sky Rider Songs (BMI)
c/o Prager and Fenton
6363 Sunset Blvd., Ste. 706
Los Angeles, California 90028

Blues Traveler Music (BMI)
see Almo/Irving

BMC (ASCAP)
Address Unavailable

BMG Music (ASCAP)
1540 Broadway
New York, New York 10036

BMG Songs Inc. (ASCAP)
8370 Wilshire Blvd.
Beverly Hills, California 90211

Bon Jovi Publishing (ASCAP)
see Polygram Music Publishing Inc.

William A. Bong Music
see Warner-Chappell Music

Bonneville Salt Flats (ASCAP)
see Warner-Chappell Music

List of Publishers

Boo Daddy (ASCAP)
see T-Boy Music Publishing Co., Inc.

Brass Crab Music (BMI)
see Post Oak

Break of Dawn Music Inc. (BMI)
c/o Real Records Inc.
PO Box 958
434 Ave. U
Bogalvsa, Louisiana 70427

Breaker Maker (BMI)
see BMG Music

Brio Blues Music (ASCAP)
see Almo Music Corp.

Bro N' Sis Music (BMI)
see Keith Sykes Music

Broken Plate Music Inc. (ASCAP)
c/o Stuart Silfen, Esq.
488 Madison Ave.
New York, New York 10022

Brooklyn Dust Music (ASCAP)
c/o Kenneth B. Anderson, Esq.
Loeb & Loeb
230 Park Ave.
New York, New York 10169

Brown Girl Music (ASCAP)
see Warner-Chappell Music

Buchu Music (ASCAP)
c/o Haber Corp.
16830 Ventura Blvd.
Encino, California 91436

Buffalo Prairie Songs (BMI)
see Sony Tree Publishing

Bug Music (BMI)
Bug Music Group
6777 Hollywood Blvd., 9th Fl.
Hollywood, California 90028

Bug Pie Music (BMI)
see EMI Music Publishing

Bugle Publishing (BMI)
c/o Bug Music Group
6777 Hollywood Blvd., 9th Floor
Hollywood, California 90028

Gary Burr Music (BMI)
see Tree Publishing Co., Inc.

Butter Jinx Music (BMI)
see EMI Music Publishing

C

John Cale (BMI)
c/o Chrisopher Whent Esq.
270 Madison Ave., Ste. 1410
New York City, New York 10016

Caleb Music (ASCAP)
see Gypsy Boy Music Inc.

Caledonia Soul Music (ASCAP)
see WB Music

California Phase Music (ASCAP)
c/o Gelfand, Rennert, O'Neil & Haga
man
1025 16th Ave. S.
Ste. 202
Nashville, Tennessee 37212

Canvas Mattress
see Almo/Irving Music

Careers-BMG
see BMG Music

Eric Carmen (BMI)
Address Unavailable

Casadida (ASCAP)
see EMI Music Publishing

Cass County Music Co. (ASCAP)
c/o Breslauer, Jacobson & Rutman
10880 Wilshire Blvd., Ste. 2110
Los Angeles, California 90024

Chappell & Co., Inc. (ASCAP)
see Warner-Chappell Music

RuPaul Charles Music (BMI)
see EMI Music Publishing

Charm Trap Music (BMI)
see EMI Music Publishing

Jolene Cherry Music (ASCAP)
see Warner-Chappell Music

Chesca Music (BMI)
see EMI Music Publishing

Chrysalis Music Group (ASCAP)
9255 Sunset Blvd., No. 319
Los Angeles, California 90069

Chrysalis Songs (BMI)
see Chrysalis Music Group

Chyna Baby Music (BMI)
see EMI Music Publishing

Cinderful (BMI)
see Chrysalis Music Group

Clark's True Funk Music (BMI)
see EMI Music Publishing

Claude A. Music (ASCAP)
see Chappell & Co., Inc.

CLT Music (ASCAP)
see All Nations Music

Club Zoo Music (BMI)
see Seventh Son Music

CMI America (ASCAP)
1102 17th Ave. S.
Nashville, Tennessee 37212

Co-Heart Music (BMI)
1103 17th Ave. S.
Nashville, Tennessee 37212

Linda Cobb (BMI)
1100 17th Ave. S.
Nashville, Tennessee 37212

Coburn (BMI)
see Bug Music

Colden Grey Music (ASCAP)
Grubman, Indursky, Schindler & Gold
152 W. 57th St.
New York, New York 10019

Colgems-EMI Music (ASCAP)
see EMI Music Publishing

Edwyn Collins Music (ASCAP)
see EMI Music Publishing

Janice Combs (ASCAP)
see EMI Music Publishing

Justin Combs Music (ASCAP)
see EMI Music Publishing

Command Performance Music (ASCAP)
see MCA Music

Complete Music (England)
Address Unavailable

Controversy Music (ASCAP)
c/o Ziffren Brittenham & Branca
2121 Ave. of the Stars
Los Angeles, California 90067

Don Cook (BMI)
see Sony Tree Publishing

Cota Music (BMI)
see Warner-Chappell Music

Deborah Cox Music (BMI)
see EMI Music Publishing

Creation Music (BMI)
see Sony Music

CRGI (BMI)
c/o CBS (Sony Records)
666 5th Ave.
New York City, New York 10103

Crimson Music
see BMG Music

Criterion Music Corp. (ASCAP)
6124 Selma Ave.
Hollywood, California 90028

Mike Curb Productions (BMI)
948 Tourmaline Dr.
Newbury Park, California 91220

D

Mark D. Music (BMI)
see Sony Cross Keys Publishing Co. Inc.

Daddy Rabbitt Music (ASCAP)
see Almo/Irving

D.A.R.P. Music (ASCAP)
see Diva One

Dead Arm Music
see Almo/Irving

Dead Man's Hat Music (ASCAP)
see EMI Music Publishing

David Dedderer (ASCAP)
see EMI Music Publishing

Deep Blue Something Music (ASCAP)
see Warner-Chappell Music

Def American Songs (BMI)
16 W. 22nd St.
New York, New York 10010

Desmobile Music Inc. (ASCAP)
c/o C. Winston Simone Mgmt.
1790 Broadway, 10th Fl.
New York, New York 10019

Deswing Mob (ASCAP)
see EMI Music Publishing

Diamond Cuts Music (BMI)
see Walt Disney Music

Diamond Storm Music (BMI)
see EMI Music Publishing

Diamond Struck Music (BMI)
see MCA Music

Difficult Music (BMI)
c/o Beldock, Levine & Hoffman
565 5th Ave.
New York, New York 10017

Diggin in the Crates Music (ASCAP)
see EMI Music Publishing

Walt Disney Music (ASCAP)
500 S. Buena Vista St.
Burbank, California 91521

Diva One (ASCAP)
Gelfand, Rennert & Feldman
c/o Michael Bivens
1880 Century Park E., Ste. 900
Los Angeles, California 90067

Divided (BMI)
see Zomba House

Dixie Stars Music (ASCAP)
see Hori Pro Entertainment Group

Dog Dream (ASCAP)
Box 483
Newton Centre, Massachusetts 02159

Buddy Doiwer Music (BMI)
see EMI Music Publishing

Dollarz N Sense Musick (BMI)
see Sony Music

Door Number One
see Polygram Songs

D.R. (ASCAP)
see Famous Music Corp.

Dream Catcher Music (ASCAP)
see Sony Music

Dream Team Music (BMI)
see Sony Music

Duchess Music Corp. (BMI)
1755 Broadway, 8th Fl.
New York, New York 10019

Dyad Music, Ltd. (BMI)
c/o Mason & Co.
400 Park Ave.
New York, New York 10022

Dyinda Jams Music (ASCAP)
see Warner-Chappell Music

E

Ecaf (BMI)
  see Sony Music

Ecstasoul Music (ASCAP)
  see Human Rhythm

Edisto Sound International (BMI)
  see CRGI

Edition Beam Music
  see Warner-Chappell Music

El Viejito (BMI)
  see Sony Music

Emdar Music (ASCAP)
  see Texas Wedge

EMI-April Music (ASCAP)
  see EMI Music Publishing

EMI-Blackwood Music Inc. (BMI)
  see EMI Music Publishing

EMI Music Publishing
  810 7th Ave.
  New York, New York 10019

EMI Songs Ltd.
  see EMI Music Publishing

EMI Tower Music (BMI)
  see EMI Music Publishing

EMI U Catalogue (ASCAP)
  see EMI Music Publishing

EMI Variety Catalogue (ASCAP)
  see EMI Music Publishing

EMI-Virgin (ASCAP)
  see EMI Music Publishing

EMI-Virgin Songs (BMI)
  see EMI Music Publishing

Endless Soft Hits (BMI)
  1802 Massachusetts Ave., Ste. 22
  Cambridge, Massachusetts 02138

Enjoi Music (BMI)
  see EMI Music Publishing

Seamus Ennis Music (BMI)
  see Sony Music

Entertaining Music (BMI)
  541 Manhattan Ave.
  New York, New York 10017

Evelle Music (BMI)
  see Warner-Chappell Music

Excellent Classical Songs (BMI)
  see Roshashauna

Exile Music (BMI)
  7820 Wingate Park Cove
  Memphis, Tennessee 38119

EZ Duz It (ASCAP)
  see EMI Music Publishing

F

Famous Music Corp. (ASCAP)
  10635 Santa Monica Blvd.
  Ste. 300
  Los Angeles, California 90025

Farrenuff (ASCAP)
  see Longitude Music

Feat Music (ASCAP)
  c/o Loeb & Loeb
  10100 Santa Monica Blvd., Ste. 2200
  Los Angeles, California 90067

Fifth Floor Music Inc. (ASCAP)
  Attn: Martin Cohen
  6430 Sunset Blvd., Ste. 1500
  Los Angeles, California 90028

First Release Music Publishing (BMI)
  6124 Selma Ave.
  Hollywood, California 90028

Firstars Music (ASCAP)
  see Almo/Irving

Five Piece Set Music (ASCAP)
  see Warner-Chappell Music

List of Publishers

Flying Rabbi Music (ASCAP)
c/o Jason Finn
915 E. Harrison, Ste. 201
Seattle, Washington 98102

Flyte Tyme Tunes (ASCAP)
c/o Margo Matthews
Box 92004
Los Angeles, California 90009

FMP Music
see Warner-Chappell Music

Foggy Jonz Music (ASCAP)
see Polydor International

For Ya Ear (ASCAP)
see EMI Music Publishing

Foreign Imported (BMI)
8921 S.W. Tenth Terrace
Miami, Florida 33174

Fortunate Moon Music (BMI)
see Almo/Irving

48/11 Music (ASCAP)
c/o MFC Management
1428 S. Sherbourne Dr.
Los Angeles, California 90035

4MW Music (ASCAP)
see Zomba Music

Fox Film Music Corp. (BMI)
c/o Twentieth Century Fox Film Corp
PO Box 900
Beverly Hills, California 90213

Freedom Songs Music (BMI)
see EMI Music Publishing

Friends and Angels Music (ASCAP)
see Walt Disney Music

Full Keel Music (ASCAP)
9320 Wilshire Blvd., Ste. 200
Beverly Hills, California 90212

Full Volume Music (BMI)
see EMI Music Publishing

Furious Rose (BMI)
500 5th Ave., Ste. 2800
New York, New York 10110

G

Garlicky Music (ASCAP)
see Almo/Irving

Get Loose Music Inc. (BMI)
PO Box 1198
Jacksonville, Florida 32201

Ghetto Jam (ASCAP)
see Chrysalis Music Group

Gifted Pearl (ASCAP)
see EMI Music Publishing

Beverly Glen Publishing (ASCAP)
c/o Loeb and Loeb
Attn: D. Thompson
10100 Santa Monica Blvd.
Ste. 2200
Los Angeles, California 90067

Glenwood Music Corp. (ASCAP)
see EMI Music Publishing

Globe Art Music (BMI)
see EMI Music Publishing

GMMI Music (ASCAP)
see Sony Music

Godhap Music (BMI)
see EMI Music Publishing

Golden Reed (ASCAP)
see New Clarion

Golden Rule Music (BMI)
c/o J.C. Cobb
5353 Indiana Ave.
Chicago, Illinois 60615

Gone Gator Music (ASCAP)
c/o Zeiderman, Oberman & Assoc.
500 Sepulveda Blvd., Ste. 500
Los Angeles, California 90049

Goodie Mob Music (BMI)
see Organized Noize

Gouda Music (ASCAP)
c/o Don Bachrach
1515 N. Crescent Heights Blvd.
Los Angeles, California 90046

Grand Alliance (ASCAP)
c/o Southern Grand Alliance Music
1710 Grand Ave.
Nashville, Tennessee 37212

Grand Royal Music (ASCAP)
see EMI Music Publishing

Great Cumberland Music (BMI)
see MCA Music

Green Daze (ASCAP)
see Warner-Chappell Music

Green Fingers Music (BMI)
Address Unavailable

Al Green Music (BMI)
Box 456
Millington, Tennessee 38053

Greenburg Music (BMI)
see Sony Music

Groove 78 Music (ASCAP)
see Almo/Irving

Gypsy Boy Music Inc. (ASCAP)
Mitchell, Silberberg & Knupp
1800 Century Park, E.
Los Angeles, California 90067

H

Rick Hall Music (ASCAP)
PO Box 2527
603 E. Avalon Ave.
Muscle Shoals, Alabama 35662

Hame Waje Music (ASCAP)
see All Init

Hanes, Hill & Valentine Music
see Polygram Music Publishing Inc.

Harnia Music (ASCAP)
see Warner-Chappell Music

Harrington Music (ASCAP)
see EMI Music Publishing

Hayes Street Music (ASCAP)
see Almo Music Corp.

Head Cheese (ASCAP)
see PRI Music

Head with Wings Music (BMI)
see Pubco Music

Heathalee (BMI)
see EMI Music Publishing

Hidden Planet (BMI)
see Famous Music Corp.

High Steppe (ASCAP)
Fitzgerald Hartley
50 W. Main St.
Ventura, California 93001

Hit & Run Music (ASCAP)
1841 Broadway, Ste. 411
New York, New York 10023

Hollenbeck Music Co. (BMI)
c/o Ernst & Whinney
1875 Century Park, E.
Los Angeles, California 90067

Holmes Creek Music (BMI)
see Almo Music Corp.

Honest Music (ASCAP)
Attn: Craig Wasson
4133 Kraft Ave.
Studio City, California 91604

Honey Music (BMI)
see BMG Music

Hori Pro Entertainment Group (ASCAP)
1819 Broadway
Nashville, Tennessee 37203

List of Publishers

Hot Cha Music Co. (BMI)
130 W. 57th St.
Ste. 12B
New York, New York 10019

Hot Head Ltd. (England)
Address unavailable

House of Fun Music (BMI)
1348 Lexington Ave.
New York, New York 10128

Howlin' Hits Music (ASCAP)
PO Box 19647
Houston, Texas 77224

Hudson Bay Music (BMI)
1619 Broadway
New York, New York 10019

Human Boy Music (ASCAP)
see Warner-Chappell Music

Human Rhythm (BMI)
see Chrysalis Music Group

Humble Artist (ASCAP)
see Polygram Music Publishing Inc.

I

Ides of March Music Division (ASCAP)
Wayfield Inc.
1136 Gateway Ln.
Nashville, Tennessee 37220

Ignorant (ASCAP)
see Warner-Chappell Music

I'll Show You Music (BMI)
see Bug Music

Indian Love Bride Music (ASCAP)
Siegel, Feldstein, Duffin, & Vuylst
1500 Broadway, Ste. 1400
New York, New York 10036

Innocent Bystander Music (ASCAP)
207 1/2 1st Ave. S.
Seattle, Washington 98104

Insofaras Music (BMI)
see Sony Music

Interscope Pearl (BMI)
see Warner-Chappell Music

I.R.S. Music (BMI)
see First Release Music Publishing

Irving Music Inc. (BMI)
360 N. LaCienega Blvd.
Los Angeles, California 90048

Chris Isaak Music Publishing (ASCAP)
P.O. Box 547
Larkspur, California 94939

Island Music (BMI)
6525 Sunset Blvd.
Los Angeles, California 90028

It Made a Sound Music (BMI)
see EMI Music Publishing

Itchy Putschy (BMI)
see Warner-Chappell Music

Itself Music (BMI)
see EMI Music Publishing

J

Jalma Music (ASCAP)
see Island Music

Jay-Boy Music Corp.
c/o Seymour Straus Herzog & Straus
155 E. 55th St., Ste. 300B
New York, New York 10022

Lorrie Jayne (BMI)
1000 18th Ave.
Nashville, Tennessee 37212

Jazz Merchant Music (ASCAP)
see Zomba Music

JEC Publishing (BMI)
8025 Melrose Ave.
Los Angeles, California 90046

Jeddrah Music (ASCAP)
c/o Lopey & Gonzaley
attn: Ellen Burke
15250 Ventura Blvd.
Penthouse 1220
Sherman Oaks, California 91403

Jizop Music (BMI)
see Almo/Irving

Jobete Music Co. (ASCAP)
attn: Denise Maurin
6255 Sunset Blvd.
Los Angeles, California 90028

Patrick Joseph (BMI)
119 17th Ave. S
Nashville, Tennessee 37203

Joshua's Dream Music (BMI)
see Warner-Chappell Music

John Juan (BMI)
see Famous Music Corp.

Jumping Cat Music (ASCAP)
see Write Treatage Music

Justin Publishing Co. (ASCAP)
see EMI Music Publishing

K

K-Man (BMI)
see Sony Music

Victoria Kay Music (ASCAP)
see BMG Music

Kear Music (BMI)
1635 N. Cahuenga Blvd.
Los Angeles, California 90028

Keeno Music (BMI)
see Ruthless Attack Muzick

R. Kelly Music (BMI)
see Zomba Music

Kicking Bird (BMI)
see Famous Music Corp.

Jay King, IV (BMI)
c/o Mitchell Silberberg
11377 W. Olympic Blvd.
Los Angeles, California 90064

Diana King Music (ASCAP)
see EMI Music Publishing

Kingsley Gardner's Nation of Soul Music
(ASCAP)
see EMI Music Publishing

David Kitay Music (BMI)
see Famous Music Corp.

Dee Klein Music (BMI)
see Little Reata

Kmel Music (BMI)
see Sony Songs

L

Lac Grand Music (BMI)
see Sony Music

Sonny Landreth Music (BMI)
see BMG Music

Lanni Tunes (BMI)
see Sony Tunes

LaRue Two Music (BMI)
see Almo/Irving

Late Hours Music (ASCAP)
see EMI Music Publishing

Lazy Kato Music (BMI)
see EMI Music Publishing

Leeds Music Corp. (ASCAP)
c/o Mr. John McKellen
445 Park Ave.
New York, New York 10022

Left Right Left Music (BMI)
see Bug Music

List of Publishers

Lenono Music (BMI)
The Studio
1 W. 72nd St.
New York, New York 10023

Leo Sun Music (ASCAP)
see EMI Music Publishing

LFR Music (ASCAP)
2541 Nicollett Ave. S.
Minneapolis, Minnesota 55404

Rebecca Lilla Music (ASCAP)
see Famous Music Corp.

Linder Ltd. (BMI)
Address Unavailable

Little Beagle Music (ASCAP)
see BMG Music

Little Big Town (BMI)
see MCA Music

Little Dakota Music (BMI)
c/o Java Lina
808 19th Ave. S.
Nashville, Tennessee 37203

Little Miss Music (ASCAP)
see EMI Music Publishing

Little Pitt Music (BMI)
see Warner-Chappell Music

Little Reata (BMI)
see Irving Music Inc.

Livingsting Music (ASCAP)
see Malaco Music Co.

LL Cool J Music (ASCAP)
attn: James Todd Smith
PO Box 219
Elmont, New York 11003

Loco De Amor (BMI)
1775 Broadway
New York, New York 10019

Long Acre Music (SESAC)
see Warner-Chappell Music

Longitude Music (BMI)
c/o Windswept Pacific Entertainment
9320 Wilshire Blvd., Ste. 200
Beverly Hills, California 91212

Loon Echo Music (BMI)
see Zomba Music

Jack Lord Music (ASCAP)
c/o Lisa Thomas
321 High School Rd. NE, Ste. 304
Bainbridge Island, Washington 98110

Love This Town (ASCAP)
see MCA, Inc.

Lovely Sorts of Death Music (BMI)
see EMI Music Publishing

Lowery Music Co., Inc. (BMI)
3051 Clairmont Rd., N.E.
Atlanta, Georgia 30329

Ludakris (ASCAP)
see BMG Music

Lunn Music Music (ASCAP)
see Warner-Chappell Music

Luscious Jackson Music (ASCAP)
see EMI Music Publishing

M

Maanami Music (ASCAP)
see EMI Music Publishing

Maclen Music Inc. (BMI)
see ATV Music Corp.

Mad Castle Music (BMI)
see Polygram Music Publishing Inc.

Mad Dog Winston Music (BMI)
see Warner-Chappell Music

Major Bob Music (ASCAP)
1109 17th Ave. S
Nashville, Tennessee 37212

Malaco Music Co. (BMI)
PO Box 9287
Jackson, Mississippi 39206

Malamution Music (BMI)
see Warner-Chappell Music

Aimee Mann
see You Can't Take It With You

M. Marie Music (BMI)
11377 W. Olympic Blvd.
Los Angeles, California 90064

Marjer Publishing
see Stage-Screen Music, Inc.

Martians Go Home Music (BMI)
see BMG Music

Matanzas Music (ASCAP)
see Warner-Chappell Music

Maverick (ASCAP)
see Warner-Chappell Music

Maximum (Germany)
Address Unavailable

Maypop Music (BMI)
Box 121192e Cavender
702 18th Ave.
Nashville, Tennessee 37212

MCA, Inc. (ASCAP)
1755 Broadway, 8th Fl.
New York, New York 10019

MCA Music (ASCAP)
1755 Broadway
New York, New York 10019

McJames Music (BMI)
see Almo/Irving

Mega Music (BMI)
see BMG Music

Melodisc Music (ENGLAND) (BMI)
Address Unavailable

Mercer Street Music (BMI)
see Songs of Polygram

Dave Mergenda Music (ASCAP)
see Sony Music

Metered Music, Inc. (ASCAP)
Peter Matorin
c/o Beldock Levine & Hoffman
99 Park Ave.
New York, New York 10016

Midwest Moon Music (BMI)
see Bug Music

Mighty Nice Music (BMI)
see Polygram Music Publishing Inc.

Mighty Three Music (BMI)
c/o Earl Shelton
309 S. Broad St.
Philadelphia, Pennsylvania 19107

Mijac Music (BMI)
see Warner-Chappell Music

Mike & Alice Music (ASCAP)
see All Nations Music

Mile Music (ASCAP)
see Acuff Rose Music

Millhouse Music (BMI)
see Polygram Music Publishing Inc.

Mills & Mills (ASCAP)
c/o Chappell & Co., Inc.
810 7th Ave.
New York, New York 10019

Miss Bessie Music (ASCAP)
9247 Alden Dr.
Los Angeles, California 90210

Miss Blyss Music (ASCAP)
see Starstruck Writers Group

Joni Mitchell Publishing Corp. (BMI)
c/o Segel & Goldman Inc.
9200 Sunset Blvd., Ste. 1000
Los Angeles, California 90069

MJ12 Music (BMI)
see EMI Music Publishing

List of Publishers

MLE Music (ASCAP)
see Almo Music Corp.

Mo Swang Music (ASCAP)
see Def American Songs

Mo Thug Music (BMI)
see Ruthless Attack Muzick

Monica's Reluctance to Lob (ASCAP)
see EMI Music Publishing

Monkey Dog (BMI)
410 Pack Ave.
New York, New York 10022

Monster Island (ASCAP)
see Chrysalis Music Group

Montezk Music (BMI)
see EMI Music Publishing

Morganactive Music (ASCAP)
c/o Dennis Morgan
1800 Grand Ave.
Nashville, Tennessee 37212

Moriel (BMI)
see Beverly Glen Publishing

Patrick Moxey Music (ASCAP)
see EMI Music Publishing

Mumblety Peg (BMI)
see BMG Music

Murrah (BMI)
1025 16th Ave. South, Ste. 102
PO Box 121623
Nashville, Tennessee 37212

Music by Candlelight (ASCAP)
see Peer-Southern Organization

Music Corp. of America (BMI)
see MCA Music

Muy Bueno Music (BMI)
1000 18th St., S.
Nashville, Tennessee 37212

MVH Too Music (BMI)
see Almo/Irving

My Split Music (BMI)
9412 Atheston Ct.
Brentwood, Tennessee 37027

My World (ASCAP)
c/o Preston Business Mgmt.
3343 Peachtree Rd. NE, Ste. 200
Atlanta, Georgia 30326

N

Nag (BMI)
see PolyGram Records Inc.

Nelana Music (BMI)
see MCA, Inc.

Ness, Nitty & Capone (ASCAP)
see EMI-April Music

New Agency Music (ASCAP)
see Warner-Chappell Music

New Clarion (ASCAP)
Box 121081
Nashville, Tennessee 37212

New Don Music (ASCAP)
see New Haven

New Haven (BMI)
see PolyGram Records Inc.

New Hidden Valley Music Co. (ASCAP)
c/o Manatt, Phelps, Rothenberg &
Phillips
11355 W. Olympic Blvd.
Los Angeles, California 90064

New Line (BMI)
see EMI Music Publishing

New Nonpariel (BMI)
see Warner-Chappell Music

New Perspective Publishing, Inc. (ASCAP)
see Avant Garde Music

New Wolf (BMI)
see Sony Tree Publishing

New York House Music (BMI)
see Wax Head Publishing

Randy Newman Music (ASCAP)
c/o Gelfand, Rennert & Feldman
1880 Century Park, E., Ste. 900
Los Angeles, California 90067

Night Garden Music (BMI)
see Warner-Chappell Music

Night Rainbow Music (ASCAP)
see Warner-Chappell Music

Nike's Rap Music (BMI)
see Chrysalis Music Group

Nineteenth Hole Music (BMI)
see Maypop Music

Ninth Street Tunnel Music (ASCAP)
see EMI Music Publishing

Nomad-Noman (BMI)
see Warner-Chappell Music

Not of This World Music (ASCAP)
see Polygram Music Publishing Inc.

Notable Music Co., Inc. (ASCAP)
Cy Coleman Enterprises
200 W. 54th St.
New York, New York 10019

Novalene Music (BMI)
c/o Pat Vegas
PO Box 1129
Studio City, California 91604

Now Sam I Am Music (BMI)
see Warner-Chappell Music

N2D Publishing (ASCAP)
PO Box 121682
Nashville, Tennessee 37212

Nu Rhythm & Life Music (BMI)
see Better Than Your Music

Nu Soul Music (BMI)
see Almo/Irving

Nuthouse Music (ASCAP)
see Warner-Chappell Music

NYM (ASCAP)
see Warner-Chappell Music

O

O/B/O/Itself (ASCAP)
see Almo/Irving

October Project (ASCAP)
see Famous Music Corp.

Of (ASCAP)
see PolyGram Records Inc.

Oji's Music (BMI)
see Def American Songs

Old Boots Music (ASCAP)
see EMI Music Publishing

Old Crow (BMI)
10585 Santa Monica Blvd.
Los Angeles, California 90025

One Four Three
see Warner-Chappell Music

Orange Bear Music (BMI)
Div. of Sunshine Entertainment
627 N. Rossmore, Ste. 312
Los Angeles, California 90004

Orbisongs (ASCAP)
see EMI Music Publishing

Organized Noize Music (BMI)
3340 Peachtree Rd. NE, Ste. 2120
Atlanta, Georgia 30326

Original Hometown Street Music (BMI)
see Square West

Orisha Music (ASCAP)
see Warner-Chappell Music

159

List of Publishers

Ozzy Osbourne Music (ASCAP)
see EMI Music Publishing

Out of Pocket Music (ASCAP)
see Warner-Chappell Music

P

Paltime Music (BMI)
see Polygram Music Publishing Inc.

Shawn Patrick Music (BMI)
see Famous Music Corp.

Paul & Jonathan Songs (BMI)
1330 Dog Creek
Kingston Springs, Tennessee 37082

Peace Pourage Music (BMI)
see Sony Songs

Pearl White (BMI)
see EMI Music Publishing

Peer Five Music (BMI)
see Leeds Music Corp.

Peer-Southern Organization (ASCAP)
810 7th Ave.
New York, New York 10019

Peermusic Ltd. (BMI)
see Peer-Southern Organization

Dan Penn Music (BMI)
see Maypop Music

Pepperstash Music (ASCAP)
see Warner-Chappell Music

Pettibone (ASCAP)
see Kear Music

Pickled Fish Music (ASCAP)
see Write Treatage Music

Pigfoot Music (ASCAP)
PO Box 130
Point Reyes, California 94956

Pink Jelly Music (BMI)
see Chrysalis Music Group

PJA Music (ASCAP)
see BMG Music

Plainclothes Music (BMI)
see PolyGram Records Inc.

Play One Music (BMI)
see Rightsong Music

Plunkies (BMI)
see EMI Music Publishing

Polydor International
see Polygram Songs

Polygram International (ASCAP)
1416 N. LaBrea Ave.
Los Angeles, California 90028

Polygram Music Publishing Inc. (ASCAP)
Attn: Brian Kelleher
c/o Polygram Records Inc.
810 7th Ave.
New York, New York 10019

PolyGram Records Inc. (ASCAP)
810 7th Ave.
New York, New York 10019

Polygram Songs (BMI)
810 7th Ave.
New York, New York 10019

Ponder Heart Music (BMI)
see Almo Music Corp.

Pookie Bear (ASCAP)
PO Box 121242
Nashville, Tennessee 37212

Post Oak (BMI)
see Sony Tree Publishing

Powhatan Music (BMI)
see Leeds Music Corp.

PRI Music (ASCAP)
see Polygram Music Publishing Inc.

Privet Music (ASCAP)
see Walt Disney Music

160

PSO Ltd. (ASCAP)
see Peer-Southern Organization

Psychohead Music (ASCAP)
see Warner-Chappell Music

Pubco Music (BMI)
Times Bldg., Ste. 200
Ardmore, Pennsylvania 19003

Pulpit Rock Music (BMI)
see Polygram Music Publishing Inc.

Purdell Publishing (ASCAP)
411 E. Randolph St.
Glendale, California 91207

Pure Songs (ASCAP)
see Screen Gems-EMI Music Inc.

Purple Crayon Music (ASCAP)
see Sony Music

R

Rag Top (BMI)
9820 Lindhurst St.
Oakland, California 94603

Ramecca Music (BMI)
see BMG Music

Rampal (BMI)
see Warner-Chappell Music

Ranger Bob Music (ASCAP)
see Polygram Music Publishing Inc.

Raw Poo Music
see EMI Music Publishing

Realsongs (ASCAP)
Attn: Diane Warren
6363 Sunset Blvd., Ste. 810
Hollywood, California 90028

Red Brazos (BMI)
Box 163870
Austin, Texas 78716

Red Cloud Music Co. (ASCAP)
15250 Ventura Blvd.
Penthouse 1220
Sherman Oaks, California 91403

Regent Music (BMI)
110 E. 59th St.
New York, New York 10022

Nadine Renee Music (BMI)
19370 Collins Ave.
Miami Beach, Florida 33160

Rhett Rhyme Music (ASCAP)
see BMG Music

Rick's Music Inc. (BMI)
see Warner-Chappell Music

Rightsong Music (BMI)
see Warner-Chappell Music

Rising Sons Music, Inc. (BMI)
811 16th Ave.
Nashville, Tennessee 37203

Ritz Rights Music (BMI)
see EMI Music Publishing

Rodsongs (ASCAP)
see Almo Music Corp.

Roland/Lentz (ASCAP)
c/o Roland Vasquez
924 W. End Ave., Ste. 1
New York, New York 10025

Rondor Music Inc. (ASCAP)
see Almo Music Corp.

Rope and Dally Music (ASCAP)
see EMI Music Publishing

Roshashauna (BMI)
533 Madison St., Ste. 3
Hoboken, New Jersey 07030

Rob Roy West Music (BMI)
see Of

Rubber Band (BMI)
see Warner-Chappell Music

Rude Corps Music (ASCAP)
see Warner-Chappell Music

Ruthless Attack Muzick (ASCAP)
3126 Locust Ridge Circle
Valencia, California 91354

Rye Songs (BMI)
see Sony Music

S

Saja Music Co. (BMI)
see Warner-Chappell Music

Samosonian Music (ASCAP)
see Warner-Chappell Music

Larry Sanders Music (BMI)
see Polygram Music Publishing Inc.

Kevin Savigar (ASCAP)
see Peer-Southern Organization

SBS Productions (ASCAP)
see Warner-Chappell Music

Scarlet Moon Music (BMI)
see CMI America

Scarlet's Sister Music
see Almo/Irving

Schizo Music (ASCAP)
c/o Pedell
156 W. 56th St.
New York, New York 10019

Don Schlitz Music (ASCAP)
PO Box 120594
Nashville, Tennessee 37212

Schmoogietunes (BMI)
see MCA Music

Scrap Metal Music (BMI)
see EMI Music Publishing

Screen Gems-EMI Music Inc. (BMI)
6255 Sunset Blvd., 12th Fl.
Hollywood, California 90028

Scribing C-Ment Music (ASCAP)
see Write Treatage Music

Second Decade Music (BMI)
c/o TWM Management
641 Lexington Ave.
New York, New York 10022

Second Wave Music (ASCAP)
see Walt Disney Music

Erick Sermon
see Warner-Chappell Music

Seven (BMI)
see Zomba House

Seventh Son Music (ASCAP)
Box 158717
Nashville, Tennessee 37215

Allen Shamblin Music (ASCAP)
see Almo Music Corp.

Shapiro, Bernstein & Co., Inc. (ASCAP)
Attn: Leon Brettler
640 5th Ave.
New York, New York 10019

Tom Shapiro Music (BMI)
see Sony Music

Short Dolls Music (BMI)
see Almo/Irving

Showbilly (BMI)
see Sony Tree Publishing

Sierra Home (ASCAP)
see AMR

Silver Fiddle (ASCAP)
c/o Segel & Goldman Inc.
9200 Sunset Blvd., Ste. 1000
Los Angeles, California 90069

Paul Simon Music (BMI)
1619 Broadway
New York, New York 10019

Siquomb Publishing Corp. (BMI)
c/o Segel & Goldman Inc.
9348 Santa Monica Blvd.
Beverly Hills, California 90210

Siren Songs (BMI)
c/o Gelfand, Rennert & Feldman
Attn: Babbie Green
1880 Century Park, E., No. 900
Los Angeles, California 90067

Sixteen Stars Music (BMI)
see Dixie Stars Music

Skinny White Butt (ASCAP)
see Warner-Chappell Music

Skull Music (BMI)
c/o Cavaricci & White Ltd.
120 E 56th St., Ste. 1150
New York, New York 10022

Skunk Deville (BMI)
General Delivery
Bexar, Arkansas 72515

Slam U Well Music (BMI)
see Warner-Chappell Music

Slow Dog Music (BMI)
c/o Geronimo
1 Camp St., Ste. 2
Cambridge, Massachusetts 02140

Slow Flow Music (ASCAP)
see EMI Music Publishing

E. O. Smith (BMI)
1990 Bundy Dr., Ste. 200
West Los Angeles, California 90025

Snow Music
c/o Jess Morgan & Co., Inc.
6420 Wilshire Blvd., 19th Fl.
Los Angeles, California 90048

So So Def Music (ASCAP)
see EMI Music Publishing

Sold for a Song (ASCAP)
see MCA Music

Songs of All Nations Music (BMI)
see All Nations Music

Songs of Castada (ASCAP)
see Warner-Chappell Music

Songs of Polygram (BMI)
see Polygram International

Songwriters Ink (BMI)
see Texas Wedge

Sony Cross Keys Publishing Co. Inc.
c/o Donna Hilley
PO Box 1273
Nashville, Tennessee 37202

Sony Music (ASCAP)
550 Madison Ave.
New York, New York 10022

Sony Songs (BMI)
see Sony Music

Sony Tree Publishing (BMI)
1111 16th Ave. S.
Nashville, Tennessee 37212

Sony Tunes (ASCAP)
see Sony Tree Publishing

Soul on Soul Music (ASCAP)
see EMI Music Publishing

Soundbeam Music (BMI)
see Full Keel Music

South Mountain Music Corp. (BMI)
1631 Broadway, 2nd Fl.
New York, New York 10019

South of Soul Music (ASCAP)
see Warner-Chappell Music

Space Potato Music Ltd. (ASCAP)
1290 Avenue of the Americas
No. 3230
New York, New York 10019

Special Rider Music (ASCAP)
PO Box 860, Cooper Sta.
New York, New York 10276

163

List of Publishers

Mark Alan Springer Music (BMI)
see EMI Music Publishing

Bruce Springsteen Publishing (ASCAP)
c/o Jon Landau Management, Inc.
Attn: Barbara Carr
136 E. 57th St., No. 1202
New York, New York 10021

SPZ (BMI)
see EMI Music Publishing

Square West (ASCAP)
see Howlin' Hits Music

Stackola Music (BMI)
see Warner-Chappell Music

Stage & Screen Music Inc. (BMI)
see Unichappell Music Inc.

Stage-Screen Music, Inc. (BMI)
c/o Careers Music, Inc.
Attn: Mr. Billy Meshel
8370 Wilshire Blvd.
Beverly Hills, California 90211

Stallion Music Inc. (BMI)
see Tree Publishing Co., Inc.

Starstruck Angel (BMI)
see EMI Music Publishing

Starstruck Writers Group (ASCAP)
PO Box 121996
Nashville, Tennessee 37212

Stazybo Music (BMI)
c/o Will Bratton
611 Broadway, Ste. 422
New York, New York 10012

Steveland Music (ASCAP)
4616 Magnolia Blvd.
Burbank, California 91505

Stiff Shirt (BMI)
see Warner-Chappell Music

Stone Jam Music (ASCAP)
see Warner-Chappell Music

Stranger Music Inc. (BMI)
c/o Machat & Kronfeld
1501 Broadway, 30th Fl.
New York, New York 10036

Stroudacaster (BMI)
see EMI Music Publishing

Suds City Music
Address Unavailable

Super (BMI)
see Zomba House

Superhype Publishing (ASCAP)
see Walden Music, Inc.

Sure Light Music (BMI)
see Polygram Music Publishing Inc.

Suzi Joe Music (BMI)
1411 Lipscomb Dr.
Brentwood, Tennessee 37027

Swag Song Music (ASCAP)
5 Bigelow St.
Cambridge, Massachusetts 02129

Keith Sykes Music (BMI)
c/o Keith Sykes
3974 Hawkins Mill Rd.
Memphis, Tennessee 38128

T

T-Boy Music Publishing Co., Inc. (ASCAP)
c/o Lipservices
1841 Broadway
New York, New York 10023

T-mo Music (BMI)
see EMI Music Publishing

Taking Care of Business Music (BMI)
see Warner-Chappell Music

Taylor Rhodes Music (ASCAP)
210 Lauderdale Rd.
Nashville, Tennessee 37205

TCF Music (ASCAP)
see Warner-Chappell Music

Tee Tee
see EMI Music Publishing

Tentative Music (BMI)
3125 Chesnut St.
New Orleans, Louisiana 70115

Terilee Music (BMI)
see Sony Tree Publishing

Texas Wedge (ASCAP)
11 Music Square East
Nashville, Tennessee 37212

That's a Smash Music (BMI)
see Sony Cross Keys Publishing Co. Inc.

They Might Be Giants Music (ASCAP)
232 N. 5th St.
Brooklyn, New York 11211

30 Waldo Music (ASCAP)
see All Nations Music

Thomahawk Music (BMI)
see BMG Music

Three Boys from Newark (ASCAP)
see PolyGram Records Inc.

Three Pounds of Love Music (BMI)
see Warner-Chappell Music

Threesome Music Co.
6100 Wilshire Blvd.
Ste. 1500
Los Angeles, California 90048

Thunderspiels Music (BMI)
see Bug Music

Tikki Merm Music (ASCAP)
see Almo/Irving

Tintoretto Music (BMI)
see EMI Music Publishing

Tizbiz Music (ASCAP)
see Diva One

TLE Music (BMI)
see Sony Music

To the T Music (BMI)
15445 Ventura Blvd, Ste. 316
Sherman Oaks, California 91403

Tokeco (BMI)
see Polygram Music Publishing Inc.

Tony! Toni! Tone! (ASCAP)
see PRI Music

Tops N Bottoms Music (BMI)
see Warner-Chappell Music

Tosha Music (ASCAP)
see EMI Music Publishing

Traveling Zoo (ASCAP)
see Beginner Music

Tree Publishing Co., Inc. (BMI)
see Sony Tree Publishing

Tricky Track Music (BMI)
113 Abbottsford Gate
Piermont, New York 10968

Triple Gold Music (BMI)
see Warner-Chappell Music

TRO-Essex Music, Inc. (ASCAP)
10 Columbus Circle, Ste. 1460
New York, New York 10019

True Science Music (BMI)
see Warner-Chappell Music

Truly Soothing Elevator Music (BMI)
see Warner-Chappell Music

Turkishman
Address Unavailable

12 AM (ASCAP)
see PolyGram Records Inc.

Twelve & Under (ASCAP)
see EMI Music Publishing

Two Tuff-Enuff Music (BMI)
see Almo Music Corp.

Tyde (BMI)
see Sony Music

List of Publishers

Tyrell Music Group (BMI)
8295 Sunset Blvd.
Los Angeles, California 90046

U

Undeas Music (ASCAP)
see EMI Music Publishing

Underground Connection Music (ASCAP)
see Warner-Chappell Music

Unichappell Music Inc. (BMI)
see Warner-Chappell Music

V

Van Hurst Place Music (ASCAP)
see MCA Music

Vanderpool Music (BMI)
see Famous Music Corp.

Velvet Apple Music (BMI)
c/o Gelfand
1880 Century Park E., Ste. 900
Los Angeles, California 90067

Vibe Crusher Music (BMI)
see Almo/Irving

Virgin Songs (BMI)
see EMI Music Publishing

W

Walden Music, Inc. (ASCAP)
see Warner-Chappell Music

Jamie Walters Music (ASCAP)
see Almo/Irving

Warner-Chappell Music (ASCAP)
10585 Santa Monica Blvd.
Los Angeles, California 90025

Warner Source Music (ASCAP)
see Warner-Chappell Music

Warner-Tamerlane Music (BMI)
see Warner-Chappell Music

Warneractive Songs (ASCAP)
see Warner-Chappell Music

Wax Head Publishing (BMI)
2168 SW 98th Pl.
Miami, Florida 33190

WB Music (ASCAP)
10585 Santa Monica Blvd.
Los Angeles, California 90025

Webo Girl (ASCAP)
see House of Fun Music

Weenie Stand Music (ASCAP)
see Warner-Chappell Music

Weowna Music
see Bug Music

Wet Sprocket Songs (ASCAP)
901 3rd St.
Ste. 407
Santa Monica, California 90403

Whonga Music (ASCAP)
see EMI Music Publishing

Why Walk (BMI)
Address Unavailable

Wild Country Music (BMI)
see Warner-Chappell Music

Windswept Pacific (ASCAP)
4450 Lakeside Dr., Ste. 200
Burbank, California 91505

Wing It
Address Unavailable

Wino Funk Music (BMI)
see Warner-Chappell Music

Wocka Wocka Music (BMI)
see Sony Music

Wonderland Music (BMI)
see Walt Disney Music

Woodsongs (BMI)
see Ruthless Attack Muzick

Woolnough Music Inc. (BMI)
1550 Neptune
Leucadia, California 92024

World of Andy's Music (ASCAP)
see Sony Music

Bill Wray Music
see Polygram Music Publishing Inc.

Wrecking Ball Music (BMI)
5111 Greenwood Ave. N.
Seattle, Washington 98103

Write Treatage Music (ASCAP)
207 1/2 1st Ave. S.
Seattle, Washington 98104

Wu-Tang Music (BMI)
see BMG Music

Zakk Wylde Music (ASCAP)
see EMI Music Publishing

Y

Yellow Dog Music Inc. (ASCAP)
see Hudson Bay Music

Yellow Elephant Music
see Sony Music

Yessup Music Co. (ASCAP)
10100 Santa Monica Blvd., Ste. 2340
Los Angeles, California 90067

You Call These Songs (BMI)
see Warner-Chappell Music

You Can't Take It With You (ASCAP)
9034 Sunset Blvd., Ste. 250
Los Angeles, California 90069

Young Legend (ASCAP)
see Chrysalis Music Group

Dionne Yvette (BMI)
see Sony Music

Z

Zanesville Music (BMI)
see Almo/Irving

Zen of Iniquity (ASCAP)
see Almo Music Corp.

Zomba House (ASCAP)
137-139 W. 25th St, 8th Floor
New York, New York 10001

Zomba Music (ASCAP)
137-139 W. 25th St., 8th Fl.
New York, New York 10001

ISBN 0-8103-6428-X

90000

9 780810 364288